the amazing next

waking up to the journey ahead

the amazing next

brock morgan

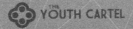

The Amazing Next

Copyright © 2015 by Brock Morgan

Publisher: Mark Oestreicher
Managing Editor: Tamara Rice
Cover Design: Adam McLane
Layout: Marilee R. Pankratz
Creative Director: Mrs. Robinson

ISBN-13: 978-1942145097
ISBN-10: 1942145098

The Youth Cartel, LLC
www.theyouthcartel.com
Email: info@theyouthcartel.com
Born in San Diego
Printed in the U.S.A.

This is dedicated to all of our students at **Trinity**.
Thank you for your friendship and for how wide-open
you've been for this **amazing journey**.
I have loved every second, and every page
in this book has had you in mind.
I have written this for you and for every student
who is longing for more
and is ready for the **adventurous,**
expectant life with the GOD who is on the move.

CONTENTS

life is either
a daring adventure
or nothing.
helen keller
the open door

Call It an Opener

It was early one Saturday morning, way before dawn, and I heard, "Brock, wake up, lets go!" I wasn't sure where we were going but I was always ready for an adventure. And if my friends had the crazy idea to get up this early, it would have to be for a good reason. They told me to pack a small backpack, a little food, and grab my jacket and boots. I was out the door within seconds. We drove for a few hours, and then finally we approached the base of a mountain. They told me that this hike would lead us to the most amazing summit view imaginable, but it would take all day. The goal was to get to the top by sunset and then camp overnight. So we started up through the valley along the river and toward the snowy summit.

If I were being honest, I'd tell you the hike wasn't just full of wonder and delight but also full of pain and despair.

If I were being honest I'd tell you that after about three or four hours, my legs felt like someone was hitting them with a hammer. My feet became like sandbags, terribly heavy, and crying out for a soak in a hot bath. If I were one hundred percent truthful, I'd tell you that I wanted to quit, started crying, and almost radioed in for a rescue plane to pick me up.

But I'm usually too tough to confess this.

I do love adventure, so I find myself on the trail like that more times than I'd like. Journeying up the trail—heck, even down the trail—is painful and difficult. You are very likely to be pushed to the brink. But the truth is, it's kind of like life. Life is a journey and there will be ups and downs along the way—some of them painful and difficult. It can be a tough hike to traverse.

But I've always loved stories of adventure, and it's actually why I started following Jesus. It's why I've kept following Jesus. Yet throughout my journey with God, people have kept trying to turn this expectant life with Jesus into something else altogether. Like a bait and switch. At the beginning they promised that following Jesus was the best life I could possibly have, only to then turn and list all the things I could no longer do. They've tried to make me a good boy, civil, a person who doesn't make too much noise.

But I want to warn you about something right here at the beginning of this book, just so that you know what you're about to read. I want you to know what you're getting into here, so here it is, here's the warning: **This book is not about helping you become a good civil person who doesn't make too much noise.**

Heck, it's not even about keeping your faith, although I think Jesus *has* made me into a better person and I *have* kept my faith.

But many times youth workers, parents, and mentors worry about graduates making mistakes and losing their faith, so they go out and buy the "right" books and pass them off as gifts to make sure these things don't happen. This might even be the reason someone handed you this little book. (But if that's the case, they didn't read this page ... obviously.)

So let me just say, if you're annoyed by the people around you worrying that you'll lose your faith, I feel your pain. I remember my parents being worried about me. When I finally got baptized I was truly concerned that they just might hold me under the water until I really, *really* repented, just so that I wouldn't eventually "lose my faith." And to be honest, I actually did give my parents a lot to worry about. I was kind of ADD with my faith. Some days God felt closer to me than my own skin, but most of the time I felt utterly alone, completely isolated, like God was further from me than the most distant planet. And so as I got older I would hear people talk about young people "losing" their faith and how I needed to "keep" it, but that never made sense to me. That kind of talk never resonated with me.

For example, when I got married I fully intended to "keep" being married to my wife, and I've always considered what I had with Jesus to be kind of like that—a really close relationship. I mean, why would I lose a relationship that's important to me?

Besides, that whole word choice wasn't even appealing. "Keeping" something didn't seem like a great adventure. But the reality is that if I want to keep my marriage or my relationship with God, intentional choices do have to be made and commitments need to be *kept* along the way.

Still I've always wanted adventure with God, transformational experiences, life-altering callings, daily struggles followed by amazing rescue plans. I've just wanted what pastors have always told me Jesus offers: life to the fullest. How can I have that?

If that's what you are longing for, then keep reading.

And I've got a second warning about what this book is not: **It's not a book that will tell you what *not* to do.** I never liked anyone telling me what not to do, and honestly I still don't. In fact, I hate it, even if it's something I don't want to do anyway. (How crazy is that?)

I played college basketball, and over my years of playing I never liked it when a coach would say, "Just stop doing that!" Okay, I'd think, but what do you want me *to do*? Because telling me what *to do* is better. I can do something with that. And I've seen how over the centuries people have tried to turn this beautiful relationship with God into a sin management tool. Like faith is all about not doing things.

And I mean we all know what *not* to do, but what are we supposed *to do* on Saturday nights? What am I supposed *to do* with my time, my life?

Now there are times, of course, when we need to be told, "Hey, stop doing that!" Like when a kid puts her finger in a light socket. But you almost never overhear people telling little kids what *to do* with their fingers. (Maybe this is why so many little kids are walking around with their fingers in their noses, ears, and mouths!)

I remember my youth pastor saying things like, "Don't smoke, or drink, or chew, or go with girls who do." Well, all those things that he said I shouldn't do actually sounded kind of good to me—especially since he just told me not to do them.

See, when we turn faith into a rigorous rule-following religion, we lose everything Jesus was trying to initiate. In fact, I believe the last thing he wanted to do was to start another "religion." Jesus looked around and he saw people who were not living life to the fullest. He saw that many were living lives they never truly wanted. He wanted to set them free into the wide open spaces, where they could breathe and grow and become.

When I was in college, my friends and I started cliff-jumping. Just down the road from our college campus were these amazing cliffs along the Tennessee River. One night a large group of us headed off to do some night-jumping. When we arrived and looked over the fifty- and eighty-foot portions of the cliff, I remember having mixed feelings: like total fear with complete excitement. I was just so nervous to jump out into the night sky. I remember my friends doing the countdown—"Three! Two! One! Jump!"—and soaring through the air out into the blackness. But, man, I couldn't even see the water. I had no idea as I was flying through the air, when I would even land.

But ...I remember the anticipation.
  I remember the fear.
  I remember the adrenaline rush.
  I remember the excitement.
  I remember feeling totally alive.
  And I remember finally taking that leap and soaring.

I want to soar. I want to wake up with the expectation that God has something remarkable ahead. I don't even need to know what it is, I just want to be awake, alive, and aware of what he's doing, so that I can be a part of it.

So I've given you two warnings as to what this book is *not* about, but I also need to tell you what this book *is* about. So here you go: **It's about life. It's about truly living—living life without**

fear, worry, or anxiety. I know what those things are about. I know fear well. I've spent many days with anxiety. I have fallen into prisons of addiction and had many hang-ups along the way. I know where these things have gotten me, and I'm tired of them.

So in case my intention for this book wasn't clear the first time, let me reword it: **This book is about freedom, imagination, and wonder.**

It's about finding God in both the loud and in the quiet. And it's about breaking through the status quo, the one-direction current of our culture, and learning to live life with Jesus in the midst of all of the noise.

Hopefully in reading these pages you will discover who you really are and what you were actually made for. But at the same time, I realize that you are living life the way you are living it. I realize this is just a book and that books rarely transform us. So, my prayer isn't that this book changes you at all. My prayer is simply that you meet Jesus in the midst of reading it and that you discover the one who is always at work and offering you a life that requires your complete, crazy trust.

I was walking the other day with a high school student. It was chilly but very pleasant out; and as we strolled through the shopping district of my city, she told me that she just felt hopeless. She said she had a few good friends and that she does have a lot of fun on the weekends at parties and whatnot. But she told me that just below the surface, she feels like she's completely alone. Like winter is setting in and maybe there's not much of a future for her; like everything around is dying and slowly growing cold. Maybe that's why she doesn't allow herself to slow down, to be still. If she can just stay busy then she won't have to deal with this winter of her life. And as we walked through the bustle of the streets I wondered what Jesus might be up to in this little conversation. Maybe he was lifting our heads, trying to make us aware of him. Trying to show us both that there really was a better way to live.

As I write this, I'm looking outside of my window. It's really cold outside, but I know spring is coming. The long winter will soon be gone and the built-up snow over these few months will eventually melt away into the water that will help usher in new life, turning everything vibrant with color. And I sense something new on the horizon, something unexpected. Deep down I feel an excitement brewing for what might be.

Great days are ahead and adventure awaits.

life is a blank canvas,
and you need to
throw all the paint on it you can.
danny kaye

chapter 1

So Now What?

So my band of brothers and I headed onward and upward toward the summit view. When we got to what I thought was the top it was underwhelming, to say the least. I thought, "This is what we spent all day climbing to see?" But then my friend told us we weren't quite there yet. We had to cross a pipe from our side of the cliff across a vast chasm to reach the other side. We were up so high that when I looked over the edge it took my breath away. I could barely see the ground below.

"No way am I going to cross that pipe!" I said. But then my friends started making their way across one by one, holding onto a flimsy looking rope to maintain their balance. They all made it easily, every single one of them—talk about peer pressure. I had to do it now, my reputation as an adventurer was on the line.

So I stood with one foot on the pipe and the other foot firmly planted on the ground. A radical choice had to be made. I had to decide, and so I did. I lifted my foot up from the ground and placed it next to my other foot on the pipe. I could feel my heart beating through my shirt as I scooted across, doing my best not to look down into the sheer drop below me. Little by little I made my way across this fifteen-foot pipe and then finally leaped from the pipe to the ground on other side. (I felt totally relieved until I realized I'd have to cross back over it again on the way back.)

Together we made our way up a wooded incline and through the forest, which ended at the edge of the mountain. And finally there it was, the summit view. It was everything my friends had described to me and so much more. We just stood there in the silence, the wind blowing gently, the sky beautifully lit with reds, deep oranges, and soft yellows across a blue backdrop as the sun slowly descended behind the mountains.

It was like I could breathe for the first time in my life.
     All of the world seemed to be perfect in that place.

I have always been drawn to people who see life as an adventure. I've rarely gone over to a friend's house to play X-Box for hours on end. Not that there's anything wrong with that, it's just that my friends have always seemed to live differently, and they've kind of dragged me along for the ride. I think that at the core of who we are there is this longing to truly live. Living life to the fullest is something we all desire. Every single one of us wants to live a life worthy of a movie script. It's just that many of us have not made the strategic and thoughtful choices necessary in order to make some of those moments happen.

Choices to step off of the edge, choices to jump from the cliff into the river, choices to get out of bed and do something meaningful. Choices to live out a calling even when it is uncomfortable. Most of us just wake up and life kind of happens to us. Living fully aware and on purpose requires a certain kind of mindset for sure.

I also really like people with strong opinions. Honestly, indifference has always kind of annoyed me. You know, people who just don't seem to care. I've been drawn to people for most of my life who make choices and live life purposefully headed in that direction. They care deeply and passionately about where they are going and what they are doing. Their choices matter.

But most of us make hundreds of choices every day and we probably are completely unaware of them. We choose when to wake up, what to do with our mornings, who to hang out with, and what to eat   just name a few. (Speaking of what to eat, I just entered a contest with some of my friends to see who could lose weight and get into better shape the fastest. We began this contest this morning with a weigh-in. (I work with the other guys in this little contest, so I've been strategically placing sweets in their offices all day long. I'm hoping to sabotage their success and win this little contest. *Choices.*)

Like I was saying, there really are so many seemingly inconsequential choices that we make every moment of every day. So many of the "big" choices have been made by others in your life. But you, my friend, are moving from being the captive of other people's choices to the decider of your own fate. Bigger than when to wake up and whether or not you should brush your teeth. We are moving into a time when big, important life-altering choices are being made by YOU.

There is a college student I know who has decided to take a gap year starting this next semester. His goal is to join in the fight with the abolition movement. It makes him angry to think that there are millions of people who are enslaved today. At this moment there is a little girl somewhere in the world who has been taken from her family. She is forced to do unspeakable things with her body for horrible men everyday. This makes my college friend angry. Angry enough to actually do something about it. He doesn't want to be a part of another generation who says they follow Jesus but never actually get off of the couch. He wants to rescue that little girl and other little ones just like her. He wants his life to count.

God says:

> I have given you the choice between life and death, between blessings and curses. Now I call on heaven and earth to witness the choice you make. Oh, that you would choose life, so that you and your descendants might live!
>
> Deuteronomy 30:19 (NLT)

I love this passage because it's right there in black and white, and it's actually extremely moving for me. Every one of us longs to make deep, thoughtful, and lasting impressions. We all want to make a difference. Every person wants to experience joy and love and avoid negativity and drama. This passage shows us that God, rich in compassion, has favored us, he has given us freedom to choose life or death. God looks at us and says, "You pick, you choose: What do you want in this moment?" If we choose to go with him, to do life with God, deeper meaning can be found.

But there's a whole other side to this power to choose. You can choose to dabble in death. In fact, sin really isn't these little individual things we do that are "naughty." It really is a choice to live in the land of death, to participate with what steals life from us and breaks our relationships with others. So that's the actual choice. Will I participate today with life or with death? Where will I truly live today? Will I live in the land of fear, the region of anger, and the kingdom of insecurity and addiction? Will I participate in what is not bringing life to the world?

What's so cool about this verse is that God is actually pleading with us, begging us to choose life, to choose freedom. "Oh, that you would choose life, so that you and your descendants might live!" It reminds me of Jesus' words when he was asking people to follow him, and if they did they would find life, life to the fullest.

> GOD is actually pleading with us,
> begging us to **choose life**,
> to choose freedom.

One of my favorite movies right now is a movie called, *Django Unchained*. It's a 2012 American epic written and directed by Quentin Tarantino. This brilliant, moving, and quite disturbing movie stars Jamie Foxx and Christoph Waltz. The story is set in the Deep South and the Old West in the 1800s when slavery was alive and well. The film follows a slave by the name of Django (Jamie Foxx) and an English speaking German bounty hunter named Shultz (Waltz) posing as a traveling dentist. The plot begins when Django is offered his freedom if he will help Shultz capture three outlaws. If Django agrees to help him, not only will it mean he gains his own freedom but it will also give his wife her freedom too. So Django has to make a decision, which seems like no decision at all. He, of course, chooses freedom.

Early in the film a conversation takes place between three slaves and this bounty hunter. The bounty hunter kills a slave trader and injures the other. He looks at the three slaves that were being held captive and says to them, "So as I see it, when it comes to the subject of what to do next, you gentlemen have two choices.

First, once I am gone you could lift the horse off of that slave trader and carry him to the next town to get help … Or, second, you could unshackle your selves, take that rifle, put a bullet in his head and bury the two of them deep, and then head to a more enlightened area of the country. But the choice is yours."

The choice really is theirs. Neither way is easy, even the choice that might mean their freedom is a difficult one. Every choice is a seed you sow, and those seeds produce fruit in your life—either for life or for death. And if we want to have the life Jesus died to give us—an abundant life full of peace and joy, even in times of grief; full of true meaning and purpose, even in the midst of suffering—we have some critical choices to make.

There have been days that I have chosen the way of death. I have made decisions that have led me into the dark places of life, places like C.S. Lewis created in *The Chronicles of Narnia*, where there was "winter but never Christmas." We all know despair and hopelessness, we all know brokenness and sometimes we take ourselves there. We've all made choices that we regret.

A while back I was at a coffee shop with a college sophomore. I asked him if he had any regrets. Without hesitation he said, "No way. I've never regretted anything I've ever done."

Now you have to know something: This kid really should have had some regrets. If I were him, I'd have a lot. He'd hurt many girls, including one teenager he'd left pregnant; he was on drugs and couldn't get off of them; and to top it all off, his mother was the one who introduced him to drugs in the first place. There were certainly some things to regret. He was broken, hurting, and longing for a better way. That's why he was sitting across from me with a chai tea in his hand. But for whatever reason, he couldn't allow himself to experience regret. I think maybe it's not a politically correct thing to have regrets these days, but I sure have them.

Yes, I've learned from my mistakes, but my mistakes have done damage to the people around me and made my journey more difficult than it had to be. For that I have deep regret. And that really might be the point: Choose a life of death, of loss, of regret, of lost years OR choose life, purpose, mission, joy, and live today to the fullest.

So what if we chose life?
    What if we choose life on this day, in this moment?
    What if we made a choice for wholeness, for health, for
        friendship, for service, for love, for adventure?
    What if you called someone and told that person how much
        he or she means to you?
    What if you apologized to someone that you hurt at some
        point in the past?
    What if you went for a hike?
    What if you wrote a poem, a song, or created something
        beautiful?
    What if you grabbed some friends and went to a concert and
        danced and enjoyed life together?
    What if you texted someone younger than you and you en
        couraged him or her? You know what it's like growing up
        today, in this world.
    What if we lived on purpose, conscious of our choices,
        today?
    What if we did something that truly mattered?
    What if?

here's to freedom,
cheers to art.
here's to having
an **excellent adventure**
and may the stopping never start.
jason mraz

chapter 2

FREE: A Poem

I lay on my bed with arms stretched out, looking at the ceiling,
A mind full of nothingness, waiting for something to happen.
Boredom is quite a serious matter.
Clouds up above and humidity in the air,
What can I do on a day like this?
Then ...
Something hits the glass.
Tap.
Curiosity shoots my body straight.
Tap. Tap. Tap.
Drops slide down gently.
Excitement stirs in me.
I know just what to do.
Barefooted, I run.

Laughing,
Dancing,
Jumping,
Playing,
Giddy,
Free.
I spin,
Mouth open wide, looking to the sky,
joy in my heart,
filling my mind with childhood memories
of rainy days like these.
I may be soaked from head to toe,
I don't care.
Eyes may be watching,
I don't care.
People may be judging,
I don't care.
I am free.
I am free to live.
The rain may stop, but must I?

By: Dancin Morgan

chapter 3

Put Words to It
(And Maybe a Picture Too)

How do you feel about the freedom, the hope, and even the fear in your journey ahead? Write your own poem or simply enter your thoughts—hey, you can even put your feelings into artwork here. Go ahead and fill these pages.

Group Chat | Is College Really Better Than High School?

Whenever I hear adults tell high school kids how the high school years are the greatest time of their lives, I'm always baffled. Actually, I feel sad for those adults, because they obviously stopped living when they left the walls of their high schools. I can tell you that for me and for most of my friends, life just keeps getting better and better. But I guess it's all dependent upon the choices you make.

Below is a conversation with some great college students who are experiencing the joy of the college years. Their names are Evan, Zoe, Jonny, Heather, Casey, and Krista, and I hope what they have to say is an encouragement to you.

Let's talk about the differences between high school and col-

lege. What do you miss or not miss? Is college really better than high school?

Zoe: For me, college has felt like an answer to all of my deepest prayers and desires in high school. I'm learning in classes that I'm truly interested in; I'm surrounded by other Christians; I live in a city that lives and breathes music—almost everything about my college experience has been exactly how I always dreamed. It's true that college is better than high school, but it's also much harder.

I'm also pretty positive that if there were a "best and coolest parents" award, my parents would win hands down. They couldn't have dominated parenthood any more than they did. They gave me more freedom, independence, and trust than I probably deserved, and I'm a better human being because of the way they teach me and love me. But that didn't change the fact that learning to live on my own wasn't exactly the breeze that everyone makes it out to be. College is better than high school because no matter how much freedom, independence, and trust your parents gave you, college finally feels like your life.

Heather: I'm not sure what it is about college but people simply feel more free to be themselves. Far away from the judgment of old teachers, friends, and parents, I've found that the freedom you experience in college has a lot to do with being free to discover yourself and make your own decisions. Let me explain: In college, you are free to make the mistake of staying up late talking to your friends knowing you have an eight a.m. class; you are free to watch all those movies you couldn't at home because you were afraid your parents might walk in; you're free to choose to make your bed or not; you're free to make your own friends, manage your own time, try new foods ... all these things give you the freedom to make decisions without the influence of life up to this point. It's almost like you are a kid again and you get to look at ideas, places, and people from an entirely new perspective, a blank slate; but this time you can be honest about how you feel because there is no one to constantly look over your shoulder.

The other thing that makes college so different for me is how grown up I feel. There is a mental shift that happens when you enter college. Things that seemed cool when you were a senior in high school just seem silly now. For example, I was talking with one of my friends the other day and one of our other friends was talking about someone behind this person's back and my friend said, "Wow, that is just so high school." There is this realization that you are uncomfortably close to living in the real world—finding your own house, getting a job, getting married. High school seems far away and you simply learn to grow up.

Jonny: Yeah. And really, it's all about FREEEDOM! College is the kingdom of it. All of a sudden, you have all this free time to do whatever you want with people all around you who are the same age.

There are endless possibilities to create a new type of life, any life you want! There are so many different activities you can engage in, which allows you to discover what you truly love to do. For example, I've been to Salsa Club, Club Frisbee, Table Tennis Club, Meditation Club, Ukulele Club, and I plan on trying out Robotics Club next semester. It is so cool to meet different types of people by doing activities that you enjoy most.

Also, if you live on campus everything is so close together that it really isn't a hassle at all to get anywhere! Not only can you do what you want, but you do not have a set curriculum either. So you have much more freedom to do what you want when learning. I found that my relationships with people have significantly deepened as well. Having the ability to stay overnight with people all around you is truly remarkable. It makes meeting up with people outside of school so much easier and enhances the sense of community.

Krista: College is better than high school because you get to find out who you are apart from your family. You are handed a tremendous amount of responsibility and freedom, and for an independent person like me it's been so nice.

Casey: Yes, it really is your time to figure out what values, beliefs, and interests you truly have without the influence of your parents, past friends, and teachers. Stupid things that you thought mattered in high school don't anymore. Instead, college students begin to put value in real world topics rather than insignificant high school drama.

Evan: I would caution anyone to never look ahead in life and think that once a certain something happens, everything will be fixed or everything will be better. Life's a journey, and it's pretty awesome every step of the way. You've got to have the right attitude. If you think a lot of things are going wrong in high school or that life sucks now and it'll get magically better once you leave home, I have bad news for you: If all you can see are the negatives now, that will likely be the case for the next four years as well. But that being said, in college people are generally more mature, more open-minded, and you are now free to make your own decisions (if your parents had strict rules). That's cool. So is sleeping in. Dining halls and cafeteria food are less cool, as is paying for your own stuff.

Jonny: Also, since there's usually a much bigger student body, there is so much less of the high school "drama" that almost all of us had to experience. Walking around at William and Mary, I could literally wear a Halloween costume on any day of the year, and I wouldn't even feel that weird about it. Last month, I decided to play the ukulele in the cafeteria. Now how weird would that be in high school? (Okay, that might still be a bit weird in college.)

One of the best parts of college is the idea that you can completely recreate yourself. Nobody knows who you are. Any notions that people have developed about you are completely erased. You have a chance to walk deeper than you ever have with the Lord. Rely on him completely, and he will answer you.

chapter 5

College Bucket List

I have an Irish friend who once told me that a great night in Ireland is when you go to the pub with your friends, you drink a pint, you kiss a girl, and you pick a fight. Now, that is a full evening for sure!

But I spoke recently with a few friends of mine and together we put together a bucket list of things that would be fun to accomplish during the college years OR maybe by the time you are twenty-five.

I hope they inspire you to make your own list.

Go see the northern lights
Go sky-diving

Ride an elephant
Get a tattoo
Swim with dolphins
Run a marathon
Go scuba-diving
Swim with sharks
Write a book
Kiss in the rain
Kiss in the snow
Kiss at the beach
Heck, just kiss someone
Learn to surf
Go skinny-dipping
Sleep under the stars
Learn sign language
Sponsor a child through Compassion or World Vision
  and then go visit the child
Be a volunteer youth leader
Visit all fifty states
Learn to play the guitar
Smoke a Cuban cigar
Go whale-watching
Go on a multi-day canoe trip
Raise money to help an organization that rescues
  slaves
Visit Holy Trinity Brompton—an amazing church
  in London
Travel around Europe with backpacks
Float in the Dead Sea
Tell a friend about what God is doing in my life
Learn to meditate
Hold a monkey
Go to a wine tasting

My Bucket List ...

let us step into the night and pursue that flighty temptress, **adventure**.

j. k. rowling

harry potter and the half-blood prince

chapter 6

Facebooked*

I was invited to speak at a camp quite a few years ago in Oklahoma called Dayspring—a place where teenagers come every year ready to open their lives to God. One of the youth pastors there introduced me to a girl named Hanna, and after our introduction he told me that she was fighting with all her of her might not to follow Jesus. She was coming up with every reason not believe in him and was resisting with every ounce of passion. So I started praying that there would be a breakthrough, but all week she sat in the back and didn't seemed moved at all. The camp was soon over, and I thought that no connection was made inside of Hanna.

But then one day, a couple of months later, she facebooked me.

*While these emails have been edited for better clarity—and to fit into one chapter!—they really did pass between us over a period of about five years.

August 3rd, 2:57am
Hanna Wallace

I don't know if you remember me, but I met you at Dayspring. Anyway, I got one question. It seems like I'm on a streak with them these days, but in Joshua 6, God orders the people of Jericho killed, which also includes the lives of innocent women and children. What I don't get is how he could ask this if he supposedly loves everyone. And then also in Leviticus 19:18 it says love your neighbor. It's like saying two totally different things. Yeah … I just want your thoughts.

August 4th, 2:20pm
Brock Morgan

I still struggle with parts of the Old Testament. It's hard to know what God really indicated and what the people justified. That particular story is very complicated. I have to always remind myself of the bigger story. God chose a people to rise up out of the mire and be different. He gave them freedom from the brokenness that pervaded the culture and taught them how to live lives in community. The Ten Commandments alone are so freeing for a people that have just come out of slavery. You cannot take what you want from each other, you cannot murder and get away with it—God gives them dignity. The story of Jonah speaks of God as one who is slow to anger and merciful. This God is unlike any other god of the time. Then in the New Testament we look to Jesus. This is God's answer to the problem of the brokenness in the world. God sacrifices, gives everything to reveal his love to us. Though the big story shows us how we have always rebelled against God, he pursues us anyway. I am also confused by the story of Jericho. But we have to also remember that God's personality is multifaceted. Like Job we have to humble ourselves and remember that we are nothing and can not presume to know the mind of God. These will be great questions to ask him someday.

August 8th, 9:53pm
Hanna Wallace

Cool. But what I don't get is that I thought God's supposed to give grace when it comes to our sins, and it doesn't really sound like he did with them. I thought God forgives us and all that stuff.

And then why'd he have to send his son to die anyway? Couldn't he just snap his fingers or something and then bam—everything's alright and we could go to heaven in just the same way we do now?

And thanks for your answer—seriously.

August 8th, 10:31pm
Brock Morgan

We don't understand the cosmic effect of sin—it isn't just a snap-your-fingers problem. If it were, would God have sent his son to die on a cross? No way! If it was an easy fix God would have just fixed it. But it was a desperate problem that needed a desperate solution. Man wanted nothing to do with God, and love never forces someone to love back. But love can prove how amazing it is and how deep it is. And so this is what God did: dying on a cross to show us his love. But he goes even beyond the cross and continues to pursue you with his love—even at camp a couple of weeks ago he was pursuing you. That's what love is—it's relentless.

Your questions have been my questions in the past—and they are good ones. I love that you're searching and you're seeking.

August 18th, 10:09pm
Hanna Wallace

Hey, Brock. How have you and your family been? I've got another "thinker." I was wondering how the Bible can be reliable when it's written by people—and people are far from perfect. And then you have all the interpretations of it. How do we know which one is right? And some people believe if you don't believe their interpretation then you're not saved. So, how the heck are we supposed to choose?

August 18th, 10:41pm
Brock Morgan

I love the way your mind works—great questions! Okay, so there's a lot of evidence for the reliability of the Bible. First are the prophecies—things have come true that were predicted thousands of years in advance. Then there's geology—they've done digs that have proven some vital facts in Scripture (Indiana Jones stuff). The reliability is quite amazing. BUT God never intended for us to have a perfect understanding of Scripture. He wanted us to wrestle with questions and study hard and learn and talk through issues. It really is the best way to learn—not to just have all the answers but to be allowed to discover them.

But, of course, this means people might arrive at different viewpoints, which is beautiful and wonderful—diversity in our thinking is great. But we have to respect each other's viewpoints. Important, huh?

It can be small-minded for us to think our way of thinking is the only way. The different interpretations of the Bible are not typically varied on the main points—those parts are fairly clear. It's usually the minor things that people fight over, and it's really too bad. The cool thing is that we don't have to join in fights over things that don't matter anyway. The main things of Scripture are harder to argue about. Also, Scripture is an amazing ancient writing, written by people but inspired by God—it's cool stuff!

 August 25th, 7:55pm
Hanna Wallace
That makes sense. You're lucky to live up north, it's freaking hot down here—ha! Well, I was wondering about the topic of Jesus. Like, how human was he? Because one of my friends believes in the whole God thing, but I believe in praying to Jesus. So, like was Jesus really God? Or like someone consumed by God? Does that make any sense?

 August 25th, 9:02pm
Brock Morgan
I believe that Jesus was fully human and fully God—weird huh? In context, Jesus was the promised Messiah (that's what the word "Christ" actually means). He was God in the flesh, who came to do amazing things—the climax being his death and resurrection. He was and is God. He claimed to be God, believed he was God. Now only a crazy person would think this of himself, or an absolute jerk, or maybe he was a liar, or … or maybe he was actually who he said he was: He was God. If

he was crazy then I don't want to follow him; if he was egocentric and a jerk—well I don't respect him; if he was a liar—then I want nothing to do with him. So this only leaves one option for me: to believe he was who he said he was. That he wasn't crazy, a jerk, or a liar but he was God. Does this make sense?

August 25th, 11:25pm
Hanna Wallace

Sort of. But then you get into where he, like, questioned God himself and prayed to him, I guess. If he was God then what was the point of praying to God?

August 26th, 2:42pm
Brock Morgan

Praying is just talking, so Jesus continued to have a relationship with his father (God) by talking or "praying" to him. Jesus praying or having a conversation with his heavenly father doesn't mean that Jesus isn't the Messiah. This is kind of confusing because we're getting into the Trinity (God the Father, God the Son, and God the Holy Spirit—three persons—almost like three Gods ... well, kind of ... but not really). Think of Jesus having this amazing relationship with his Father—whom he has known before time even began, which is crazy to even think about. BUT Jesus came to earth out of love for us and ALSO out of obedience to his father. So of course he'd continue to say things like "not my will but yours be done." He showed true submission—not just to his father but also to us—he lowered himself and died our death. So Jesus could pray to his father and still be God himself, because there are three persons to the Godhead. He's just one of them ... hope I'm not losing you here. It's really a mystery, and we struggle with thing we cannot categorize or pin down.

December 20th, 11:06pm
Hanna Wallace

Hey, Brock. IDK if you remember, but I had asked you a couple questions over FB after camp in July. Anyways ... I had another question if you wouldn't mind answering it.

So, what if you don't know anything about Jesus, or just not much? What if someone believes in God or a god, but not Jesus?

December 25th, 2:44am
Brock Morgan

Hannah, great hearing from you. Hope you're having a wonderful week. Oh, by the way, Merry Christmas!

Hey, great questions. Paul in Romans talks about the idea that we are only held responsible for what has been revealed to us. So if you have never heard of Jesus you are not responsible for that. In other words, if a kid in Africa has never heard of Jesus but he looks at creation and thinks that there must be a good and creative God, then I believe that child will be in heaven when he dies. Many Christians might not agree with me on this one, but it seems as though Paul (who wrote most of the New Testament) thought this way.

Jesus helps make sense of it all because many religions already try to get to God without him. They do this by obeying rules and trying to be "good enough" for God. What Jesus does is create a relational bridge—through him we can be "born" into God's family. Think about a baby born in your home. Does it have to "do" anything to be loved and cared for? Or is it just loved and cared for because it was born into your home? Jesus has made a way for us to see God and our relationship with him differently. Full of enjoyment, repentance, forgiveness, extravagant love, etc., that others cannot know. Acknowledging who Jesus is and what he has done gives us such freedom and gratitude. Hell is not the reason we follow Jesus/God. His love for us is.

See God is a good God and I think you will be surprised by how many people will be in heaven (not in hell). I'm not sure who has taught you about hell, but from your questions it seems like this is a point of contention for you. The Bible barely talks about hell. In fact, we don't know who goes there (if anyone). The only thing we do know is that God created it for Satan and the demons. Some great theologians say that the only humans that will go to hell are people who hate Christ so much that they actually don't want to be a part of God's kingdom—they've actually chosen hell over heaven. Weird, I know, but there's a lot of intelligent consideration in this idea.

All this to say, I don't know much about hell at all. If anyone says they do then they are delusional. BUT I do know that God is good and we can trust him. My prayer is that no one goes there. Maybe this actually will happen—let's hope. But I trust God. He died so that no one will perish. Let's hope this is the case.

Have a Merry Christmas!

January 2nd, 11:24pm
Hanna Wallace

Okay. So that's relieving. I guess what I'm hooked up on still is whether it's even true. We studied some religions at school and some books kept saying how other religions influenced Christianity. Like their ideas about God creating earth from water and about the divine punishment of humans through floods later—some people say these other religions influenced the writers of the Old Testament. At least that's what the book we read was stating. Then you have Jewish monotheism, which "served as a basis for the development of Christianity and Islam." THEN you have Mithraism, and some people believe it came from the Persians, centuries before Christianity. It had the whole story of Mithras being born of a virgin, belonging to a holy trinity, heaven and hell, light of the world, baptism, bread and wine. What confuses me is this: If something is the truth, shouldn't it be first and not copying some other religion? Like shouldn't it have its own story? Or did the stuff that's taught in the Bible NOT REALLY happen but is just there as stories to teach morals. Cuz if that's the case, then I can see that stuff being passed down from like Mithraism or whatnot and used as "teachings." I just can't see the stories being fact or history though.

Have a great weekend with your fam!

January 6th, 11:38am
Brock Morgan

One thing we have to realize is that all truth is God's truth. When a Mormon says something that is true it's God's truth, when a Muslim says something that is true it's Gods truth, and when Mithraism teaches truth … that's right, it's God's truth too. All truth is God's truth. There is a lot of truth out there in other religions that is true and from God. This may sound controversial but, it's ridiculous to think that other religions don't contain any truth.

As you know Mithraism is very mysterious and full of controversy. There's just not a lot we know about it. But at that time, stories were circulating about the history of the world. These stories were about creation, life, death, humanity, God, etc. At that time there was a great oral tradition and religions were closer in belief systems than they are today (or than we like to say they are today). So it isn't that Judaism borrowed stories and beliefs from others, it's that as a human race we have the stories that have been passed down since the beginning of time. Some are bogus and some are true or at the very least contain truth for us. So what we have to do is be seekers of truth—no matter where it leads us. We have to be willing to go because it will eventually lead us to a better understanding of God. Why? Because all truth is God's truth.

Most Christians don't live life with humility. We think that all religions are all wrong except for Christianity, but this, I believe, is wrong thinking and very arrogant. What's cool is to think that a lot of the major religions today have a similar beginning: God created. That's a great start, heavy with truth that we can agree with.

Now the Buddhists and the Hindus understand how everything is connected, and they understand holistic thinking (mind, body soul, spirit)—this is something that we can appreciate and take as true. The Muslims understand honor and respect for God, and they understand worship and devotion—this is a truth from God that we can appreciate and hold to. And by the way, many scholars actually believe that the original Muslim scriptures indicate that Jesus rose from the dead—crazy, huh?

And Mormons love Jesus and they whole-heartedly believe in him. They understand that faith without works is dead, and this is a truth that we hold as well. We can go on and on here. I hope this isn't confusing you or frustrating you. It's just that life isn't black and white. It's full of greys and we can't say with certainty that one religion is all wrong or another is all right. It's cloudy and grey at best.

So why Christianity then? Because I believe it has a much fuller, comprehensive base of truth. It, when understood, makes sense of life and our mission on earth. Through it God is accessible and approachable. The prophecies, geography, historical evidence, extra-biblical evidence, etc., tends to point me to the truth of Jesus from Nazareth. And many major religions respect and honor him.

I have a friend who was agnostic. But he started to notice that most major religions spoke highly about Jesus Christ. So after much study he decided to become a Christ-follower. Not a "Christian" necessarily—he wasn't comfortable with that word—but he wholeheartedly believed in Jesus and studied the Bible with passion. I find this to be very cool.

Anyway, I hope this helps a bit—and it gets your mind going.

Blessings, Brock

April 21st, 11:31pm
Hanna Wallace

Hey! IDK if you remember, but I had asked you a lot of questions a while ago. Anyways, I saw you're coming back to Dayspring camp again and wanted to say: How awesome! How are you?

And here's a question to add to my list: As far as sinning … if you're sorry that you did something and ask for forgiveness but don't quit doing it … does God still forgive you?

April 22nd, 1:03am
Brock Morgan

Hey, great hearing from you! I've missed the questions.

I think the best way to answer your question is this way: In the past I have done things at times that have been hurtful to people I love. And when I hurt them I said sorry, but inside I knew I would just keep doing the same thing over and over again. I felt sorry but it became clear to them that I wasn't sorry enough to actually put them before myself. And it became clear to me that I wasn't loving them well, and inside I knew I needed to make some changes. I felt like a jerk and, in fact, I was one. I was close to losing my friend.

But God is super patient and there is no end to his love. In response to this you can live one of two ways. The first is under the mercy of God. You're sinning, but because of his mercy he withholds the cosmic consequences of your sin from you—at least for a time. Then there's another way and that's under the grace of God. It's like you've surrendered to him (you're following him) and he lavishes you with his blessings and pours out his grace on you. The second way is a much better way. It's better to receive blessings than to just have judgment withheld. Especially in the context of a relationship with God. We can put God in a place of mercy where he longs to freely bless us! I hope that makes sense.

At the same time, it's so easy to get addicted to something or find yourself in the middle of something that you can't seem to get out of. And, truthfully, you might not even want to get out of it. If this is the case, it's important to get help. We can't follow Jesus alone. It's impossible, and we need others to pull us out of the crap sometimes that we find ourselves in. I hope that helps!

By the way, I'm looking forward to camp this summer as well. Should be a blast!

Okay, let's pause for a second. I went back to that camp in Oklahoma again, and Hanna was there. On the last night she came forward and asked Jesus to be a part of her life, to lead her through this crazy life. She came to the front, and I had the honor of praying with her. It was amazing!

 July 26th, 7:13pm
Hanna Wallace

Hey! Glad to hear you got home safely. Guess what? They had me give my story today at church. It was crazy! I never thought I'd be doing that in a million years and saying what I did. Ha! Just wanted to say thanks again for all your support. I leave in a week for college. I'll keep in touch though! Hope all is well!

July 26th, 7:36pm
Brock Morgan

I'm very proud of you—I wish I could have heard it. Keep running toward God, and let me know how you're doing in school. Don't forget who you are and whose you are.

August 6th, 11:40pm
Hanna Wallace

Hey, Brock! Hope all is well. I had a question for ya. Ever since camp I haven't really partied and haven't been drinking at all or anything else. But the problem is that it just seems so boring these days. Honestly, since going from partying every day to not ... I have no idea what to do with myself. I was just wondering if you had any suggestions or advice. Cuz now that I'm gonna be on my own I have no idea what I'm supposed to do—if that makes sense? Hope you and your fam are having a great rest of the summer!

August 8th, 6:19pm
Brock Morgan

Ha—yeah, that makes sense. God is going to help you discover how to truly live—to live in freedom. But it's going to be a process. New ways of fun are going to be discovered. Just hang in there. In the meantime there is so much for you to do. Get with some friends who are running after God and hang out. Do life with them. Go hike, swim, jump off of a cliff into the river, go dance, play, head out on adventures, but do it all with the reality that God is with you!

Get involved in serving. Care for the down and out, the marginalized, the broken, the poor. Be a volunteer with a youth group (maybe middle school ministry—they are some crazy people!), join a Bible study, go to the Christian club on your campus, get super involved in things. It is so important that you not allow boredom to drag you back into the old way of life. I'll be praying for you. Please let me know how you're doing. You're the best, and God is so proud of you!

Over the months that followed, Hanna continued to aks me questions about faith, and I continued to engage her questions. The

the next summer I went and spoke again at that same camp from the first time we met, and where Hanna chose to follow Jesus, and then ...

> July 24th, 10:53pm
> **Hanna Wallace**
> Dude, Brock. Just wanted to give ya appreciation and encouragement. I've talked with several students and God's power on Wednesday night changed their lives—and mine, in a huge and life changing way honestly. Way to freaking BE BOLD and follow through with the dream man. That shows strength and passion. Hope you had a safe flight and had fun in Oklahoma. Much love, bro!

> July 25th, 10:42am
> **Brock Morgan**
> You're awesome—God used you this past week. It was so cool seeing you invest and pray over students ... SO cool! Thanks for the encouragement—it means a lot!

Our Facebook messages continued off and on throughout Hanna's college years, and here's what's great: That was just the beginning of Hanna's ministry to youth. She's pursuing ministry as a fulltime calling now, and in fact she's currently an intern on my staff.

I don't know if you saw any of your own faith journey in our exchange, but I hope you come away from it reminded to never be afraid of questions—your own or those of others.

the purpose of life is to live it,
to **taste experience** to the utmost,
to reach out eagerly and without fear
for newer and richer experience.
eleanor roosevelt
you learn by living

chapter 7

Misfits and Fish That Swallow You Whole

I've been told by my mom, my sisters, and (yes) even my wife, that I have what they call brain damage. Not the kind you get from a terrible fall or by some tragic accident. It's something else, and I have to agree with them. My problem is this: I tend not to think much before I do things.

This started almost right from the get-go. Case in point, I remember being in kindergarten and seeing a beautiful little pony-tailed girl out on the playground. The sun was out, the sky was blue, and she was radiant—just sitting there playing dolls with a friend. Of course, I had no plan or strategy to get her attention, I just knew that I wanted her to notice me.

Some boys pull pigtails or have good pick-up lines, but not me. I walked up behind her and proceeded to spit on the top of her head. (Yeah, I know. I have major issues.) You might be asking yourself, "Why in the world would he do such a thing?" Well, here's my answer: I Don't Have a Clue. To this day I can still see her turning around to look at me with shock and horror written on her face, feeling the top of her head with her hand and then screaming at the top of her lungs.

I don't think she liked it.

Here is another thing about me: As I've already mentioned, I hate being told what to do. I struggle every time someone lords his or her power over me. I feel my blood pressure rise and that vein in my forehead pops out when the "Do this! Do that!" starts flying around. Maybe you're the same?

All this to say that it is comforting to know we have things in common with each other. The human condition plagues us all as we walk through this life together. What bothers me the most is that I really desire to live well, but I can't seem to pull it together. How is God supposed to move in and through me when I am such a mess? How am I supposed to make a difference in the world, or even my school or my workplace, when I am so consumed with myself? Is our situation hopeless or is there a better way to live?

When I read stories about the followers of Jesus, it excites me. Because it seems that Jesus not only loves people with issues, he also seems to *like* them. Jesus came on to the scene and was drawn to people who were messy, broken, insecure, addicted, angry, rebellious, and had short attention spans. But they were also people who were not content with the status quo. They longed for something more, and in Jesus they found the unexpected. They found acceptance, truth, love, mission, and adventure.

They found something they couldn't find anywhere else.
See, Jesus called these superbly normal people into an amazing life of danger, to venture out into the waters of the unknown. And he was constantly challenging them to trust him, to follow him—regardless of what the crowd was doing. And this was no easy task.

> When Jesus saw the crowd around him, he gave orders to cross to the other side of the lake. Then a teacher of the law came to him and said, "Teacher, I will follow you wherever you go." Jesus replied, "Foxes have holes and birds of the air have nests, but the Son of Man has no place to lay his head." Another disciple said to him, "Lord, first let me go and bury my father." But Jesus told him, "Follow me, and let the dead bury their own dead."
>
> Matthew 8:18-22

Those who actually continued to follow Jesus, even after what seemed like crazy demands, were constantly challenged to come out from their comfort zones, to leave their daily routines, to leave behind the norm, the expected, and to gamble it all on a new way to live.

Now in Jesus' time, the rabbis taught that the normal, expected routine took precedence over everything else. For example, tending to the death of your father took precedence over sacred daily prayers. When a father died you were obligated to give him a proper burial to show him honor. So, when Jesus found one of his followers saying that he had to go and get his father's funeral together, you'd think Jesus would have been very understanding, especially since Jesus is a rabbi. But what Jesus actually says is, "You must follow right now. Not next week or even tomorrow. Now." This might just be one of the most shocking and offensive things Jesus ever said.

In the story of Jesus, I constantly get the feeling that Jesus accepts us as we are, but he never leaves us as we are. He doesn't let us get too comfortable and he demands everything. So when I gave my life to Jesus and I said to him that I would follow him anywhere and do anything he asked me to do, I didn't actually think he would take me up on it.

In this passage Jesus is saying, "If you follow me, you may not have time to bury your father, you may not have a place to sleep at night, but you will have the adventure of a lifetime. You will experience true living: LIFE the way it was meant to be lived."

> Then he got into the boat and his disciples followed him. Without warning, a furious storm came up on the lake, so that the waves swept over the boat. But Jesus was sleeping. The disciples went and woke him, saying, "Lord, save us! We're going to drown!"
> Matthew 8:23-25

The twelve disciples are these followers of Jesus who actually think that they are willing to let the dead bury the dead, that they don't mind rocks for pillows. At least, that's what they think. And so, Jesus decides to put their faith to the test.

First, He takes them out on the water …

Now hold on a minute. Water, in the Hebrew mind, always represented something wild, dark, dangerous, and evil. It represented death. You would never catch a Jewish boy playing in the deep waters of an ocean, a river, lake, or bay. Even fishermen were careful to stay in the boat.

So keeping this in mind, Jesus doesn't just take them out for a nice ride on the water. No, he leads them out into a storm. The water is crashing over the sides of the boat, the wind feels like it is going to rip them to shreds, and they begin to panic. "We are going to die!" they scream. But Jesus is asleep in the bottom of the boat.

This story reminds me of another story I first heard when I was probably four years old in Sunday school. My teacher told me about a guy named Jonah who was a follower of God, but he wasn't willing to do everything that God asked him to do. God had asked him to go to a place he didn't want to go and preach words he didn't want to say. Jonah hated the people he was to preach to. He knew that God, being good, would redeem these wretched people, the Ninevites. So, Jonah's solution was to get on a boat and head in the opposite direction of Ninevah.

Have you ever done that? You know what God is calling you to do, but you go and do just the opposite? God doesn't want you at that place, doing those things, acting the fool. He wants you here, living beyond yourself, doing amazing things. I think we've all been there—in that other place. The place of hiding. And this is exactly where Jonah finds himself.

So there goes Jonah, heading in the wrong direction, with the wrong people, at the wrong time. And because of Jonah's disobedience, God chased after him and sent a terrible storm. This storm seemed to blow in out of nowhere. Before the sailors even knew what hit them, their ship was in danger of going under. But Jonah was asleep in the bottom of the boat and wasn't even aware of this tragic circumstance. The crew, on the other hand, was desperate. Someone had to be blamed for this freak storm. After doing some hocus-pocus, they figured it had to be the guy sleeping downstairs.

They woke Jonah up, Jonah 'fessed up, and then Jonah asked God to save them. "Throw me overboard and you will be saved!" he said to the crew, and they actually did it. The wind and the waves calmed down, and Jonah was swallowed up by a great fish, which later regurgitates him out onto the shore.

Something similar is happening in our story about the disciples. They think they are going to drown, and they wake Jesus up to save them. The big difference is that Jesus is not clueless or out of control like Jonah.

When I was a much younger man, a friend of mine, Mike, and I decided to go sailing. We were staying at a beach house on the Chesapeake Bay in the middle of winter. It was very cold that day, and the wind was blowing up to sixty miles per hour. Now any rational person would know that sailing would be the last thing you'd want to do in those conditions. (The key word being "rational.") We thought this would be an amazing adventure, one for the ages. And little did we know how right we were.

We bundled up in sweatshirts and those big yellow boots that make you look like a real fisherman, got the boat ready for sailing, and took off. Without life jackets. Apparently we couldn't find any (brain damage, again), and we were too lazy to actually seek them out. As the wind caught the sail, we hit speeds I'd only gotten to in a ski boat. After just a minute or two we were about 100 yards off shore when the wind decided to lift our boat up into the air and place it back in the water upside down. I immediately began to sink under the weight of winter clothes and began ripping sweatshirts and boots off my panicked body. My lungs felt like they were going to explode as I struggled back to the water's surface.

You have to picture this for a moment: sixty mile per hour winds, big waves, freezing water, and no life jackets. I swam up to the boat and grabbed the side, looked at my friend, and said these profound words: "This is not good!" And it wasn't. Miraculously, we figured out how to flip the boat right side up and Mike heaved himself on board. But no sooner had he stood up than the wind pushed the boat fifteen yards away from me, re-flipping the whole thing and launching Mike back in the the water. The boat proceeded to cartwheel, end over end, until it was completely out of sight. I've been afraid many times before this and even since that time. But seeing the boat blow away from us was terrifying. Down deep I didn't think we were going to get out of this situation.

Now, our friends (along with my wife) had seen what had happened and came running out to the edge of the water, but were powerless to help. If they came in to get us, they too would have drowned. All they could do was call 911 and scream for us to keep swimming.

No longer under the burden of my sweatshirt and boots, I began swimming, making my way toward the shore, but no more than a couple of minutes had passed when my arms and my legs literally stopped working. The doctors told me later that hypothermia set in and my extremities just shut down in order to protect my vital organs. My arms and legs became dead weight, and I started to go under again, knowing that this was the end.

When you think you are going to die, you cannot help but become sentimental. My mind turned toward my daughter. She was two at the time and the most precious little girl in the world. I thought about her growing up without her daddy and how difficult that would be. Then I started thinking about my wife. Seriously, she is lovely. I'm amazed that she even married me. I could not imagine her living life without me and raising our daughter alone. Then it dawned on me, "She's gifted, smart, beautiful, and she'll probably remarry ..." Under the water I screamed a bubbly "NOOO!" and paddled my way to the top for one last breath before the exhaustion and hypothermia took over once again, dragging me down a third time.

I've wondered my whole life how I would respond if I had to stare death in the face. Maybe you've had similar thoughts and questions. It was really weird that last time as I was sinking to the bottom of the bay floor, knowing that my life was ending, to feel a strange peace. I said my last words. It was just a short prayer, "Lord, I place my life in your hands, and I can't wait to see you ... in like sixty seconds."

Then it hit me. Literally. Something huge hit me in the back. When I was eight years old I saw the movie *Jaws* for the first time. Immediately I started to hear the theme song in my head and thought: SHARK! Now, how ridiculous is that? I'm already drowning but this "thing" that had just bumped me really freaked me out!

I turned and placed my hands on the side of this huge beast and proceeded to kick off of it, trying desperately to get away. My intense fear shot adrenaline through my veins (which saved my life), and I began to swim away from that "thing" at an Olympic swimmer's pace. When I made it to shore, the paramedics were waiting to rush Mike and I to the hospital to be treated for hypothermia. Mike made it to shore about five minutes after me—he was a military guy in great physical shape, which probably saved his life. I told the paramedics a huge fish thing had bumped me and that it must have been Jaws. They kind of chuckled and said it was more likely a manatee. They said manatees are very curious creatures and happened to migrate to this area every year during the winter.

Now, all I have to say is this: I LOVE manatees! (As a matter of fact, I'm blown away at how God can use anyone or, for that matter, anything.)

So, here we are, back with the disciples in the storm. They are thinking that they are done for. And their solution? They wake Jesus up. But unlike Jonah, Jesus doesn't have to pray and ask God to rescue them. Jesus takes care of it himself.

> He replied, "You of little faith, why are you so afraid?" Then he got up and rebuked the winds and the waves, and it was completely calm. The men were amazed and asked, "What kind of man is this? Even the winds and the waves obey him!"
>
> Matthew 8:26-27

I love the ending of this remarkable story. They ask each other, "What kind of man is this?" In other words: "Who in the world is Jesus?"

The disciples soon discover that he is no ordinary rabbi, he's not just another teacher to follow, he's so much more. They soon discover that this isn't just a rabbi who calmed the winds and the waves, he's the God who spoke them into existence.

You know, it is easy to call Jesus "Lord" on a retreat, on a mission trip, or at church, but it's not so easy to live with him as Lord in the nitty-gritty of everyday life. We want to do our own thing, don't we? We don't like being told what to do. We want to watch what we want, drink what we want, spend our money however we want—all this without any regard to the reality that Jesus is longing to move us beyond ourselves and our hang-ups and bring us under his lordship. I think maybe that's it: We don't trust his lordship. We don't believe that following him actually will lead to a better life.

For me, that was it for most of my life. I just believed in Jesus, but I never actually followed Jesus. And to be honest, I got tired of living life like this.

I wanted more than just a belief system.

I wanted a new way to live.

I wanted to actually know Jesus and follow Jesus and be used by him.

I wanted a mission, a reason to get up in the morning that was beyond seeing my friends, and playing basketball, and going surfing.

I wanted to let the dead bury the dead, because Jesus had more important things for me to do.

I wanted to have no place to lay my head at night and jump out into the waters of the unknown.

I basically just wanted something real.

I was dying for a life worth living.

If Jesus actually is who he said he was, and if he could accept and use a ragtag group of misfits, a fish, and a manatee to change the world, then I want in on it. You too? I thought so.

Oh, and by the way, Jonah ended up saving the Ninevites from impending doom and destruction. Then he pouted about it.

Manatee Fast Facts

1. **If you are looking for a manatee, check out the shallow areas along the coast and rivers that feed into the ocean.** They are herbivores and eat on the things that are abundant there for about half the day.

2. **Manatees can weigh up to 1,200 pounds.** But while they might appear all chunky and warm at that size, looks are deceiving. Most of their body mass is stomach and intestines! When the water gets cold, they migrate to warmer water.

3. This need for warmth means some of them spend their lives going back and forth between salty and fresh water. **Manatees have an amazing internal regulation system that keeps them balanced so that the salt concentrations don't wreck their kidneys.**

4. Manatees can hold their breath for up to twenty minutes. Unlike humans who only replace ten percent of the air in their lungs, manatees replace a whopping ninety percent. **Though they can hold their breath a long time, manatees usually surface about every three to five minutes.**

5. **Unlike humans, manatees continuously replace their teeth.** Manatees lose their older teeth, which are in the front, and the new teeth grow in the back of their mouths. It's a continuous cycle for the life of the manatee.

6. Most mammals have seven neck vertebrae. The only mammals that do not are tree sloths and manatees. Scientists don't really know why this is, but the slow metabolism of the manatee might have something to do with it. **Manatees have only six vertebrae.**

7. Manatee brains are small for their size—and smooth too. Though this indicates a less intelligent critter, especially when compared to smart animals like the dolphin, they are teachable. **Manatees can perform basic tasks, are sensitive to touch, and can tell colors apart.**

8. **Baby manatees are born every two to five years to a female.** The calf stays close, nursing from the teats, and can begin eating plants in a few weeks.

9. There are no natural predators for the manatee. **Humans are the biggest risk to manatee populations.** The animals are often

killed through boat collisions, since they float near the surface of the water and move no faster than five miles an hour. (It's tough to get out of a boat's way at that speed!)

10. **Early explorers saw mermaids swimming in the ocean, but perhaps they were delusional—most likely they were encountering manatees.** (Those must've been some really homely mermaids.)

SOURCE: http://www.smithsonianmag.com/science-nature/14-fun-facts-about-manatees-180950308/#cjsQJZHpp6k-KmL1X.99

the bad news is time flies.
the good news is you're the pilot.
michael althsuler

chapter 8

Collegiate Punking 101

One of my most favorite memories about college was pulling pranks on my friends. I know it seems lame and rather juvenile, but I absolutely loved it! I went to a college that had a curfew, so a group of my friends and I would sneak out after curfew one night a week and pull pranks all around the campus. We TP'd the president's house with over a thousand rolls of toilet paper and then blamed it on our rival college. (Chaos ensued.) We put a friend's car in the middle of the administration building. We took all of the hymnals in the chapel and put them in the choir loft (people were actually really upset about this one). We took all of the furniture in the cafeteria and placed it exactly how it was supposed to be set up, only outside. Honestly, I could go on and on but instead I've gathered a list below that might appeal to you or inspire you or just maybe give you a little chuckle.

Some of the pranks below I have done and some I haven't done … yet.

Here you go:

- **Foam Bombing.** Fill a paper grocery bag with shaving cream (the foamy kind). Then slide the edge of the opening under someone's dorm room door. Then jump on the bag. After this, you should run for your life because the foam will explode and cover the entire room—ceiling, walls, and all. (It's quite amazing!)

- **Cup Walkway.** Place cups from the cafeteria or paper cups will do (you'll need A LOT) and cover the entire hallway in a dorm (or any hallway for that matter), so that people can't even see the floor and can't come or go without hitting them. It makes for great pictures as well.

- **The Crazy-Maker.** Glue all of your friend's pen tops to the pens so he can't use them.

- **Ball Pit.** Fill an entire dorm room full of ball pit balls like at McDonalds. You can do the same with magazine pages. Just make crumpled balls of the pages and fill the entire room, floor to ceiling.

- **The Belieber.** Cover a friend's wall with pictures and posters of Justin Bieber.

- **Wrap Battle.** Saran Wrap all of someone's things in their dorm room. Bed, furniture, desk, everything—if she has things on her bed, just wrap the whole thing.

- **Big Foot Needed a Toilet.** Cover someone's car completely with canned dog food. Needless to say, it won't look like dog food.

- **The Chairman.** Fill someone's entire room, floor to ceiling with chairs. You'll have to strategically put them in the room—don't stack, that's way too neat and will require more chairs.

- **Port-a-Prank.** Order a portable restroom and place it anywhere you'd like. The admin building, a dorm, the football field, the cafeteria. Get creative.

- **Paper Car.** Sticky-note a professor's entire car.

- **The Celebratory Prank.** This will take some time but, fill someone's dorm room from floor to ceiling with balloons.

- **Time Warp.** This one is if your roommate is the type of person that jets out of bed last minute, scrambles onto her bike and heads off to class. Okay, so set the alarm an hour ahead of schedule (and any other clocks in the room along with it) and then flatten the tires so she thinks she's going to be late.

- **Just Plain Mean.** Place road kill strategically on someone's bed. If you are feeling a little more adventurous, place the road kill on his chest while he is sleeping. Talk about a wake-up call.

- **Parallel Universe.** This one is a fun one. While your roommate is away at class sneak switch everything to the opposite side of the room so it's a perfect match. Then, when she brings it to your attention, seriously act as if she's crazy and it's been that way the whole time. If you can hold your composure it will be an epic punking.

- **Nowhere Fast**. Put someone's car up on the blocks about two inches. You won't be able to tell if the car is up off of the ground but when they get in to drive their car, it's not going anywhere. If it is a front wheel drive car, make sure you just do the front (or vice versa).

- **Curtain Call**. Simply sneak into the dorm shower while a friend is getting ready for another day of collegiate labor and steal his towel and clothes so he will have no other option but to grab the shower curtain. However, this may not occur to him for some time.

- **Sleep Travel**. If a friend of yours is a heavy sleeper, have her wake up in a strange place. This is so awesome when pulled off correctly.

you are wrong if you think JOY emanates
only or principally from human relationships.
GOD has placed it all around us.
it is in everything and anything we might experience.
we just have to have the **courage**
to turn against our habitual lifestyle
and engage in unconventional living.
jon krakauer
into the wild

chapter 9

William Wallace and You

When I was eighteen years old it finally happened. I was free. It wasn't that my parents were difficult or that they created a stifling environment, it's just that now I was a legal adult with no one telling me what I could and couldn't do. This is how I defined freedom.

But I have to admit something. When my parents dropped me off at college, I felt really nervous inside. Actually, I felt afraid. In fact, when they drove away and headed back home, I may have cried a little … just a little though. It's an odd thing, freedom. We long for it and then when we get it we are sometimes not sure what to do with it. Not only that, there are things always trying to steal away our freedom.

When I finally arrived at college I was full of dreams and fears with an array of conflicting and beautiful ideas. Looking back now I can see that at the time I was a bit lost and I needed someone to come along side of me—to journey with me, to show me what to do with all of this freedom. I needed a mentor, a sage to lovingly give me wisdom and vision and help me to discover who I really was.

And then something remarkable happened. After only about two weeks of college, I was being kicked out of school.

Now, this was a conservative Christian college, and I didn't think the rules applied to me. (Actually, I still kind of think rules don't apply to me.) But there I was, sitting in the office of the dean of students and he was signing my dismissal papers when, all of a sudden, in walked a professor.

He pulled the dean out of the office, and they had a heated conversation. I couldn't make out what they were saying, but I knew it was about me. After a few minutes, the dean walked back in, ripped the papers in half, and said, "You're not getting kicked out of school, but you'll need to meet with Dr. Ropp every week for the next couple of months." I breathed a sigh of relief and gave Ropp and huge bear hug. I met with him every week for those first couple of months my freshman year. Then, soon after this act of mercy, God brought another man into my life who changed my life's trajectory.

Dr. Brown was the president of the school, and one day he asked me if some of my friends and I would be willing to meet with him every Thursday morning. Of course I said yes, and so for the next four years he met with us, invested in us, and called us out of normalcy.

One day he looked at us and asked, "Do you guys know why

we're doing this? Do you know why I'm meeting with you every week?" I'm not sure if you've ever been asked a question and you know the answer is supposed to be obvious, but you really don't have a clue what the answer is. That's what this was like. So we all just kind of stared at him with blank expressions.

He said, "Well, I'm not meeting with you because I want you to become great people. You're already great people. I'm not meeting with you because I want you to believe in Jesus. You already believe in Jesus. I'm meeting with you because I see in you something remarkable. I see in you young people who could bring such amazing change to this world."

These kinds of conversations began to blow my mind. They were freeing and challenging. No one had ever spoken to me like this, except maybe my father and, honestly, it was ruining everything for me.

Yes, ruining. See, I was a P.E. major. Not because I wanted to help bring healthy habits to children around the world. I just wanted to play dodgeball for the rest of my life. But conversations like this with Dr. Brown began to cause me to rethink this whole dodgeball career. So one day I asked him, "Dr. Brown, what do you see in me? What do you think I should be doing with my life? Because what you've been teaching us recently is totally screwing up my whole plan."

He looked at me, without hesitating, and said, "Brock, you'd be a great youth worker." When he said it, I honestly think he was levitating and glowing or something, because it was like his words came right from the mouth of God. I knew immediately: That's what I'm supposed to do with my life. That was in the spring of 1991, and the very next day I started volunteering in a Young Life-type club for youth. (And you know, the cool thing about being a youth worker is that I still get to play dodgeball.)

The way I began my college experience nearly led me away from freedom, but thankfully I was rescued! I want to be really clear here: In my mind I had no idea what freedom really meant, what to do with it, or how to keep it. My choices literally led me into an overwhelming feeling of emptiness. I felt hollow and all alone. This "freedom" felt more like prison. I was without hope. See, I began doing things I didn't even want to do. Oh initially I wanted to do them, but then those things became habitual, and I couldn't even stop the things that I began to hate. Again, I needed to be rescued! Someone needed to liberate me and many times God uses people like Dr. Brown to do the rescuing.

> i had no idea what **freedom**
> really meant, what to do with it,
> or how to keep it.

When I started actually following Jesus, I realized that in doing so, he was freeing me to become my best self. Not a rule-following religious Pharisee, or no-fun-having, judgmental zealot. He was freeing me to become the person I had always truly longed to become. God wanted to empower me to actually live freely.

○———————————————————————————○

I remember being on a retreat when I was a young youth pastor and one of our students walked up to me and handed me her journal right after each of us had just had a quiet time. She asked if I would read it and let her know what I thought. She told me that during her quiet time she started writing a prayer to God but then she felt like God had responded to her, so she wrote down his words as well. She ended up recording this amazing conversation with God. I quickly scanned it and realized how incredible it was. I excitedly said to her, "Yes! Read it now, we all need to hear this!"

We were sitting in this little outdoor chapel in the foothills of California. Tall green pines surrounded it. There was an ocean view and beauty all around. Every student and adult leader there really wanted to be there, you know? We all had this longing to hear from God. And God was getting ready to speak as she began to read:

Dear Jesus,
I feel so empty, I feel broken... alone.

He answered:
I'm here. I've always been with you.

But I've made choices that have led me into a really dark place. And I haven't even spoken to you since the last retreat. I feel guilty even writing this. I feel guilty even being here, like I don't deserve to be with you.

Don't feel guilty. I understand what you're feeling.

You understand? But I have done things I swore I'd never do! I have crossed lines that I knew I shouldn't cross. And I did it knowing all along it would hurt you. I even knew it would hurt me!

You don't have to feel guilty; guilt just pulls
you away from me even further. I love you and I want
to free you from all of that.

But I don't know how to be free! I don't know how to get out of this! I don't know what to do!

You don't have to do anything, just sit here with me.
Let's just breathe and look out
at the beauty that I made for you.

Let me just give you peace right now, in this moment.

I could use some peace.

**That's not all I'm going to give you.
But let's just be here together and enjoy all of this.**

Okay. I love you Lord.

I love you too, more than you know.

She was crying as she read this, and everyone there cried along with her. It was how all of us felt. And God's words to her were also words to us. I'm always blown away how God meets us when we pursue him, when we slow down long enough and turn on the quiet. More times than not, we will find him. And when we do, his words to us are exactly what we need to hear.

One of my favorite passages in the Bible is Galatians 5:1. It's all about this beautiful, outrageous, and thrilling freedom that we find in Jesus. Look at these words: "It's for freedom that Christ has set us free. So stand firm, then, and do not let yourselves be burdened again by a yoke of slavery" (Gal. 5:1).

Life with Jesus is freeing, but many of us are satisfied with an occasional experience with him. His offer is actually for so much more. But if you're like me you go home from a mission trip, a retreat, or time away with God and you head right back into the busyness and patterns that left you empty to begin with.

The Galatian people were not sure if Jesus was enough. They were afraid to let go of their stuff and their religion, and their patterns and habits. Paul in this passage is saying that all you need is Jesus, that's it. He is the one who will lead you. He's the one who will keep you free. Just do life with him! Paul in this verse mentions the word yoke. A yoke was a wooden beam that would be carried by a farm animal like an ox. It was a sign of burdensome work and heavy labor. In fact Paul gets this analogy from Jesus when Jesus said earlier in Matthew 11:30, "My yoke is easy and my burden is light." Jesus is saying to us, who are just tired and weary, that in him we can find rest and peace. There is an ease in being with Jesus. You don't have to break your back trying to find whatever it is that you think you're looking for. In him you'll find the life of peace and joy that you've always wanted.

One of my favorite movies, and I know this will date me, is *Braveheart*. Now I realize that almost every man over the age of thirty-five will say that this movie is in his top ten; but I don't care, I love it!

I love how the main character loves his wife.
I love how he avenges her wrongful death.
I love how he fights for his freedom and the Scottish
    people's freedom.
I love the whole thing!

In fact, I want to be William Wallace or at least a William Wallace type. I want to be a freedom fighter. But it's one thing to fight for people's freedom who are being oppressed and want to be free, but how do you fight for people who don't actually think they need to be freed?

As a youth worker, this is how I feel so much of the time. I long for the students I minister to to have and to keep their freedom. To know that the way they are living is leading them straight down a path that leads to a really dark place. The excitement will wear off and leave them with addiction, pain, and brokenness. I want them to find freedom and not just get a taste of it on a retreat. I hate when I see them head home and go straight back into a yoke of slavery. I want them to live freely and lightly.

I sit around fire pits a lot. In fact, I sit around them every Tuesday night. There's a group of high school senior guys who come over every week. We talk junk, tell ridiculous stories, and eat all kinds of man-food. But we also share our lives with each other. Can I just tell you a secret? I have a dream for these guys. They may not know it, but there's a vision that I have; a reason why I am so committed to meeting with them. My goal isn't that they are perfect seventeen or eighteen year olds or that they don't make mistakes. I just want to show them how to live, how to truly live. I want them to discover that Jesus is with them all of the time. I want them to STOP doing things for him. He doesn't need them to do anything for him. And I want them to START doing things with him. I just want them to hang out with him, everyday. Because I know what hanging with Jesus has done for me. I know that when I live life aware of him, I am changed. I am who I want to be. I am free and I so want these guys to be free! I want this for every young person I minister to, and I want this for you. I want you to live freely and lightly.

For so long I was tired of trying to do the Christian faith. I spent years of my life trying to generate something on my own. I became worn out by the whole thing.

But here are Jesus' words to me and to you:

> Are you tired? Worn out? Burned out on religion? Come to me. Get away with me and you'll recover your life. I'll show you how to take a real rest. Walk with me and work with me—watch how I do it. Learn the unforced rhythms of grace. I won't lay anything heavy or ill-fitting on you. Keep company with me and you'll learn to live freely and lightly.
>
> Matthew 11:28-30 (The Message)

Freely and lightly. I like that, I long for that. But here's the cool thing—it's all yours! The gospel is not about one day getting into heaven—to believe that is to be missing the whole point. The gospel is not just a belief in what Jesus did on the cross and how he conquered death. It's a wholehearted belief that he is working and moving and on the move today. The gospel is the grand narrative that begins with creation and goes through the cross all the way to the here and now, right where you are. God is in you and in me and he is longing to wake us up to himself, even right now in this moment. He wants to destroy our religiosity and replace it with a living relationship.

Over the past year I've gotten to know this really great young man who is now heading to college. He is from the city I live in, and I first met him when he rather reluctantly came on a retreat with our youth group. He's a natural leader and encourages everyone around him. He was easy to like and fit in to the group right away. Surprisingly before he really knew us he decided to open up about his struggles in a group sharing time—struggles that you'd never know a guy like this would have. He expressed the hurt, the insecurity, and the difficulty of his past. Then he said this, "If God can become real in my life, if he can really free me from all of this junk, then man, I'm open!" And he was. He was wide open to Jesus working.

But to be honest I've seen this hundreds of times. Students on retreats are always making professions of faith toward God. Here is the big difference: He wasn't talking about experiencing God on this retreat. He was talking about back at home. He was talking about the real world. He was longing for God to free him in his daily life. He wanted more. He wanted to live well and to make a difference in the world.

See when we start actually following Jesus he wakes us up and he frees us to live this beautiful life. Our lives become about something else all together. We become the rescue plan for others. He lifts our heads, opens our eyes, and fills our mouths with his words. We become his touch, his mouthpiece, and his liberating presence in the lives of people around us. It's for freedom that God has set us free. That means we are free to set others free. This right here changed everything for me. Yes, I've been set free so that I will live freely, but I've also been set free to join God's plan for the freedom of all humanity.

Scripture's narrative is full of freedom language. We are free to actually live, thrive, and become everything our true selves are longing for.

Now don't get me wrong, this is not something that I've gotten a grasp on completely at all, but I'm moving toward it. I'm pursuing God with all of my might and with all of my strength and I'm finding him. In the midst of this pursuit, my heart is regularly filled with a peace that passes all understanding, a love that seemed impossible, and a joy that I've always longed for. Joining God in the midst of life has become my freedom. It's in following Jesus that freedom comes.

Last night a college kid called me. He said that he'd forgotten for a while who he really was. He had forgotten that Jesus was with him and offering to set him free. He said that for the past few months it was like he'd been walking around kind of asleep. So let me remind you of something: God is longing to wake us up. He wants us to live life truly awake to his freeing presence. He doesn't want you to forget that it was for freedom that he set you free.

So now we can scream at the top of our lungs just like William Wallace ...

FREEDOM!!!

it is for **freedom** that CHRIST has set us free.
stand firm, then, and do not let yourselves
be burdened again by a yoke of slavery.
galatians 5:1

chapter 10
Pro-Tip: Budget, Budget, Budget

Money was always tight for me during my college years. I was a college athlete, worked part-time jobs, was a full-time student and did ministry in my spare time. So I was super busy, a bit stressed, and money never came easy. But I did learn to keep my head above water. Every college student has tuition to pay for and books to purchase, but what about all of those other expenses? How do you budget for those?

Hopefully these little tips and resources can help.

Step 1. Add up the money coming in every month
Do you have a job? Allowance from parents? Loans?
Add up your income.

TOTAL INCOME _____

Step 2. Add up what you consistently owe every month
This is rent, car payments, membership fees, and any expense
that occurs every month and doesn't change in amount.

Note: A great idea is to figure in a savings amount each month,
even if it is only ten or twenty dollars. This way you are building
in an emergency fund and you will not be destitute if your car
needs repair.

Total FIXED Expenses _____

**Step 3. Add up your flexible and less predictable expenses
every month**
How much are you spending for necessities like gas, food, and
utilities? (Things that vary a little from month to month.) Be sure
to include an entertainment and/or hobby amount as well. Don't
forget haircuts, prescription and over-the-counter medication,
your coffee habit, etc.

Total FLEXIBLE Expenses _____

Step 4. Add up the total of all those expenses each month
Add your total fixed and total flexible expenses together.

Total FIXED Expenses _____
Total FLEXIBLE Expenses _____
Total Fixed + Total Flexible Expenses =
TOTAL EXPENSES _____

Then subtract your total expenses from total income to find out
just how tight your monthly budget really is. (By the way, your
income should be greater than your expenses. Otherwise … you
have a problem.)

So now for the moment of truth ...

TOTAL INCOME _____
TOTAL EXPENSES _____
TOTAL INCOME - TOTAL EXPENSES =
SURPLUS (OR DEFICIT) _____

Step 5. Evaluate your budget
How did you do? Are you in need of more income or are you sitting pretty? Either way, pay attention to your spending from month to month. This is a life-long skill that will literally pay off if you can learn it well. Ideally, you will have a bit left over every month and a bit in savings that you do not touch unless it's a real emergency. (No, a pair of cool kicks is not an emergency.)

Good luck!

SOURCE:
http://www.regions.com/advice/how_to_create_a_college_budget.rf

Another Budgeting Strategy: The Envelope Method

The envelope method has been a around a while, and my wife and I have used it as a married couple. Basically, once you know your flexible expenditures, you make envelopes for each category. One for groceries, one for entertainment, one for gas, etc Put the amount of allotted cash into each expense envelope. Once the cash is gone, it is gone. No more entertainment for you! (If nothing else, this will make you think before you buy that milk shake at two in the morning.)

Why do it? In an age of digital spending, money can seem intangible and abstract to us. A swipe here, a signature there But when you are literally handing over nearly five of your hard-earned dollars for that fancy cup of coffee knowing there are only ten left at home in that envelope, you might just begin to think of your money differently. (Translation: More responsibly.)

And Another Budgeting Strategy: The App

Okay, so your money is coming and going digitally and you don't trust your roommates with all your cash envelopes sitting around. Use one of these instead—or in conjunction with—the envelope method. (Because there really is an app for that!)

1. **Mint (iOS, Android)**
    Why it works: Mint connects your bank account to your spending habits. Purchases are noted by category, and it even separates ATM withdrawal amounts and bill paying from the fees of those transactions. You might be very surprised how much you are wasting each month in fees, all for the ease of withdrawing money from different banks or paying bills on-line or by phone. Maybe those fees should have bought you a hamburger (or even a new shirt) instead of lining the pockets of some bank executive. (Stick it to the man!)

    Why students like it: It keeps track of your spending by entering your purchases for you. By breaking down your spending into categories, you can decide which category needs to be cut back.

2. **Toshl Finance (iOS, Android)**
    Why it works: It's user friendly and simple. Setting it up is easy and once you do you'll get a good idea of where your money goes.

    Why students like it: Toshl allows you to set limits. For ex-ample, setting the limit of $200 per month on entertainment shows you how easy it is to go over that budget or how close you are to meeting that goal. The visual graph can be an effective reminder that you are about to spend money you do not have.

3. **Left to Spend (iOS)**
   Why it works: This app is the equivalent to the envelope method mentioned above. Simple and straight forward.

   Why students like it: If you don't want to get bogged down in details, Left to Spend is for you. Who needs graphs anyway?

4. **Check (iOS, Android)**
   Why it works: Check, like Mint, connects to all of your financial accounts. You can set reminders to pay bills and it notifies you if you are about to overdraft your account.

   Why students like it: Maybe this is the first time you are responsible for monthly bills. Maybe you are saving your memory for biology class, not paying bills. The reminders can make sure you don't end up paying unnecessary late fees.

5. **Debt Payoff Planner (Android)**
   Why it works: Yuck. Debt sucks. But the truth is we all have it, especially if we took out massive loans to pay for school. This app allows you to prioritize debt by balance, interest rate, whatever. The projected payoff date, based on your payments, is there for your viewing displeasure.

   Why students like it: If you are wondering which loan to pay off first, this app does the math for you. Efficiency at its best!

SOURCE: http://www.rasmussen.edu/student-life/blogs/college-life/awesome-college-student-budget-apps/

Budget-Friendly Ways to Get Your Text Books

chegg.com
Renting textbooks through Chegg is great. Free shipping on returned rentals and low rates for renting and purchasing. You can even extend your rental period if necessary, and they get the books to you on time.

textbooks.com
With over seven million books to choose from, you can't miss! Good prices and free shipping on orders over $25 (at the time of publication).

ecampus.com
Rent, buy, and sell at one site. Free shipping for purchases of $59 (at the time of publication) and up to half off make this site a good approach. However, the third-party sellers, usually students, can be a bit flaky about sending books on time.

bigwords.com
This site crawls the Internet for the best deals and coupons. Then it tells you where to find the books you are looking for. There is a Bigwords iPhone app for those of you buying on the go.

OTHER OPTIONS
Craigslist and Facebook are good places to advertise and ask for books. Just be careful when paying and when picking up. Do not give out more personal information than necessary (like your address and social security number).

chapter 11

Ortho-What?!

We sat there in my favorite coffee shop when he blurted out, "I can't become a Christian, Brock. Then I'd have to reject science, I'd have to vote republican. Dude, I'd have to hate gay people. I can't do it. No, I can't become a Christian."

First of all, this was a surprising statement because we weren't even talking about anyone becoming a Christian ... so that was kind of weird. Also, it was surprising because of how he was equating Christianity with all those negative things.

But I have to admit, I've had very similar thoughts. I have thought about how Christianity is being portrayed by many and perceived by some, and it's made me not want to call myself a Christian.

In fact, just this week I was driving in my car and I made a huge mistake: I turned on Christian talk radio. I know, I know. What in the world was I thinking? Let me just say this, it was a long car ride and I was really bored. But there I was driving up Highway 95 listening to an angry and, I imagine, red-faced man. This is what he said, "Christians need to stand up and fight! We need to take this country back and get rid of all of those pro-gay, anti-family, pro-evolution, pro-sex, and anti-God heathens that are destroying God's country." (I assumed he meant the United States of America.)

My second huge mistake was that I kept listening to this stupid, stupid man.

I listened for about twenty more minutes, and then my anger turned into sadness and then into deep, profound grief. Here is why: My friend at the coffee shop was talking about this exact thing. These kinds of angry, judgmental, thoughtless, and hateful words were exactly why he doesn't want to call himself a Christian.

In response to this type of angry Christian rhetoric, there are some great people who call themselves Red Letter Christians. They want people to know that they follow the red letters of the Bible—which is the color some Bibles give to Jesus' words, to make them stand out. But, unfortunately, even this hasn't solved many problems culturally. Christianity is still viewed by many as political right-wing conservatism that is anti-gay, anti-intellectualism, and pro-war—just to name a few. How did this happen? How did Jesus the Rabbi, who is known for love and grace and "turning the other cheek," become equated with all of these things? And what's interesting is that this negative view of Christianity is not just an American thing, it's also thriving in the Middle East.

Robby Butler tells of a Kuwaiti Muslim who, when asked what defined a Christian, said, "Someone who promotes immorality, pornography, and sexually oriented TV shows." Butler goes on to write, "For a Muslim to say that he has become a Christian is to communicate that he has launched into a secret life of immorality." In Kuwait they see becoming a Christian as entering into a prayerless, apostate community. What they have done, like so many of us, is linked Christianity and American culture—albeit very different aspects of that culture—together. From the perspective of a typical Muslim abroad, America is a Christian nation and is also the number one contributor to the pornography industry. This so called "Christian America" is what they credit with the downfall of global morality. Can you blame them? (See: http.//www.missionfrontiers.org/issue/article/unlocking-islam)

So why would anyone in a Muslim community want to become a Christian?

What's interesting is that most Muslims hold a very positive view of Jesus Christ. These perceptions have caused some converts to faith in Jesus in the Muslim community to remain in the mosque to worship rather than unite with the Christian church.

I find this extremely interesting and heartbreaking all at the same time. Neither a Kuwaiti Muslim who is open to Jesus nor my friend in my favorite coffee shop wants to become a "Christian," all because of how that word is being lived out.

Throughout my life I have slowly been opening my life up to Jesus, little by little. It started when I was a young boy on an Easter Sunday morning. I was about five years old and the pastor up front was talking about what Jesus had done on the cross, how he conquered death and how he wanted to have a friendship with us. At least that's how I remember it, and I know I couldn't have understood fully what he was talking about. But still, I will tell you this: I remember how I felt. In fact, I'll never forget it. I was overwhelmed with a strange presence—a warm loving presence. All of my senses were alive for the very first time in my life. I knew in that moment God was real and literally all over me. So I opened my life up to Jesus as best as a five-year-old boy could. It really didn't change much about my day-to-day life. I still was a selfish little kid who consistently fought with his older sister. But I lived in the reality that I was loved and God was with me.

When I was in second grade God made himself known to me all over again. This time a woman prayed for me and, once again, I felt God's amazing presence. I started to cry. I felt overwhelmed by God's love. These types of experiences kept happening throughout middle school, high school, and then into college. I kept running into the love and acceptance that only the God who died on a cross could show. As I got into the bigger issues and topics of life—and we'll discuss some of these in a few chapters—I discovered that we have a really big God who can handle life's most difficult and complex questions. God, in the midst of my doubts, poor behavior, and inconsistencies has always been a loving presence in my life. I know this might sound strange and you might be wondering why I'm even telling you this. Well, here it is: Why can't the followers of Jesus do to others what Jesus has been doing to me and to you and to all of humanity since the beginning of time?

There's this strange sounding word called *orthodoxy*. Basically orthodoxy is just the agreed upon beliefs that an institution or religion deems correct and true. The cool thing is that orthodoxy in the Christian faith is huge and broad and vast! And it all started with the Jewish faith, which is where the Christian faith began.

For those who followed the God of the Jews, their orthodoxy was big and wide and inclusive. See, some Jewish religious teachers taught that there was no life after death. That this life was it and once you died, you would cease to exist. Then another group taught that the moment a person died, they would enter into a resting place that they called Abraham's Bosom. Both groups were passionate about their beliefs, but neither group said the other wasn't a part of the Jewish faith. Why? I mean, their beliefs were so different, right? But their orthodoxy was big and broad and there was room enough for both groups, as well as other types of thinking on a host of other issues. Their commonality was that they both followed the God who had made himself known to their forefather Abraham and to Moses and to David and to them.

Christian orthodoxy can be boiled down to four basic tenets. While there are varying details to each one, depending on who you ask, essentially these orthodox tenets of Christianity are focused on: creation, the fall, redemption, and final restoration. (That's a much shorter list than many would imagine!) Let me explain …

Creation: It begins with the creation of all things. It could have happened over six hundred billion years or six days, ultimately it doesn't really matter. All that matters is that we agree that God did it. He created order out of chaos, life out of death.

The Fall: Then we have the fall. This is the rebellion of mankind. All you have to do is turn the news on and you will see the result of the fall. We fell away or, more accurately, turned away from an all-loving God. The result is that we've lived life without him, and sin has broken loose across the whole of creation. It's why there is poverty, war, isolation, loneliness, addiction, and dysfunction. You and I both feel it, and we hate it. I hate what it's done to me and my family and my friends. I hate what the fall has accomplished, but the amazing thing is that Christian orthodoxy tells us that this isn't the end of the story.

Redemption: The next thing that happens is redemption. Redemption in the Christian narrative is God becoming one of us. Jesus lived the life we couldn't and demonstrated his love by sacrificing himself on a cross, showing us just how far love was willing to go. Then he rose from the dead, conquering death to show us that death won't be the end of our story either. Then comes my favorite part of the story ...

Final Restoration: The Christian story ends by going back to the beginning. Every thing will be made new, order will be made out of chaos. The earth will be restored and we will be brought back into right relationship with God as revealed in Jesus. Every knee will bow before Jesus and on that day a great healing will move across the land.

I want you to notice something. I didn't say anything about abortion, war, homosexuality, science, the end of the world, or any other thing that is not a part of orthodoxy. You can be a Christian, just like being a part of Judaism, and believe all different kinds of things. In fact, most of those things I listed are not even clear. It's almost like God wants us to learn how to live in love despite our differing opinions. He wants us to use our minds and our hearts and for us to learn how to live in the midst of that tension. How do we show love to someone who disagrees with us? How do we show honor and respect to someone who not only disagrees with us but disagrees with us about something that we feel is super important?

Wouldn't it be amazing if Christians became known more for listening rather than judging? And kindness rather than broken relationships? Wouldn't be amazing if we became known for having depth and maturity? For being secure enough to be deep-spirited friends with each other even though we disagreed about potentially toxic issues—issues that tear apart other groups of people, but not us? In fact, it was Jesus who said that the world would know that he was the truth by how we love each other.

And there's this ancient saying that he coined. He said, "Blessed are the peacemakers, for they will be called children of God" (Matthew 5:9). Now, notice a couple of words in this passage:

The first word is **peacemaker**.
The second is **children**.

A **peacemaker** is not necessarily someone who is on one side or another. They don't fight until they win the battle. A peacemaker typically stands in the middle, seeing dignity and truth in both sides of the argument. They call for both sides to see what is right and good, to listen and discuss, and hopefully help the two who are in dispute find peace. This role is not easy. Being a peacemaker can actually be extremely lonely. There are so few in existence, and the world is dying for more peacemakers.

Now here's that second word: **children**.

I look like my dad, I mean, I'm his mini-me. I look like him, I laugh like him, I even think like him in a lot of ways. I remember being in middle school and realizing that I was walking around with his face. It was a bit frightening to say the least. It's not that my dad is unattractive, it's just that a kid doesn't necessarily want to be so much like their parents when they're thirteen. You know what I'm saying. But here's something else about my dad: All of my friends loved him! He was fun and smart, and every kid in my school thought he was the coolest. Kids would tell me this: "Brock, your dad is awesome!" So I started to think that maybe being like my dad wasn't so bad.

And that is what this passage is saying, that if we want to look like our Heavenly Father, if we want his DNA in our cells, if we want his heartbeat for the world, then we will stop picking fights and throwing people away. We will be the wise-thinking peace-makers. The ones who stand in between and see truth wherever it is, even if it's said by people we disagree with. I want to be like the God who has pursued me with love since I was a boy. I want to have the kind of patience and tolerance that he has shown me and the entire human race since the dawn of time. I want to look just like him!

May we be known for carrying God's heart of peace to everyone we meet.

So we sat there in that coffee shop, and I looked at my friend and said, "Dude, lots of Christians embrace science, vote Democrat, and love homosexuals and fight for their right to marry."

He looked at me like I was nuts. Then he said this, and I'll never forget it: "Brock, I think I actually really love Jesus, I just can't get around certain things that I hear Christians say."

I just looked at him and said, "Me too man. Me too."

wisdom begins in **wonder**.

socrates

chapter 12

Group Chat | What About Roommates?

I've had good roommates and I've had some pretty bad room-mates. A few I was sad to part with and one I wasn't. Here's some wisdom from some great college students—Evan, Zoe, Jonny, Heather, and Krista—on living well with roommates.

What are some tips you can offer others heading into their college years and nervous about being, getting, and keeping a good roommate? What can they do if the roommate situation isn't all they thought it would be?

Jonny: Make it a priority to talk on the phone with your future roommate at least once before going to college. This would be a great time to hear about his (or her) interests and beliefs. Come in with the expectation that your roommate's beliefs and expectations will be different than yours. Respect your roommate's ideas, even if you don't agree with them.

Zoe: I pretty much hit the jackpot with the whole freshman roommate thing, and I definitely don't take it for granted. There are some pretty bad horror stories out there, and I just thank the Lord they're not mine to tell. My roommate and I are each other's best friends in college, which is such a blessing but definitely comes with its difficulties too. The most important thing I've learned about living with another person is that it's still okay to need time alone. Living with someone is like getting a crash course on their life, personality, past, personal habits, and everything in between. Whether or not you get along with your roommate, even the most extroverted of extroverts needs a few minutes to themselves every day—and it's okay to need that.

Krista: In the past year and a half I have had nine different roommates. Living with someone is incredibly difficult and takes patience and a whole lot of grace. One thing I learned pretty quickly was that nobody is perfect and expecting your roommate to be perfect will only result in bitter feelings. If you have an issue with something your roommate is doing, talk about it, to the roommate, IN PERSON. Make time for your roommate, even if you're not best friends. It will make living with them a lot more enjoyable.

Evan: Just don't be a jerk. My roommate and I aren't best friends. He's an engineer, I'm undecided. I exercise and play pick-up sports with my friends, he doesn't. He likes cheesy pop music, I don't. He likes to relax and do work on weekends, and I like to go out and see people. But we are courteous to each other, we know we both live in the same room, and we respect each other. So we're able to see eye to eye. So far, we haven't had a single disagreement that wasn't immediately resolved because of that mutual respect.

Jonny: I had a friend last year that had an interesting roommate situation. One of his conflicts was that one of the roommates had a very different ideal temperature than him. During the winter, this guy's roommate would keep the window open at night to let the cold air in. One night it got so cold that my friend had to get out of bed and put on all of his warmest clothes and curl himself up into a tight ball. Since he couldn't reach the window without waking his roommate up, he had a pretty uncomfortable night! Who is at fault? It doesn't matter. Yes, the other roommate might be inconsiderate, but it was still my friend's responsibility to tell him that this window 24/7 rule was not working out too well. If he'd communicated to his roommate, the whole thing could have been avoided.

Heather: I love my roommate, and we get along really well. I think the reason for this lies in that in the beginning of the year we sat down for five minutes and made a list of dos and don'ts, which now graces the wall of our room—like a roommates' agreement. Although it was extremely awkward at the time, because we barley knew each other, I cannot tell you how many arguments it has saved us from over the last semester. I know exactly what she expects of me and I of her. On the off-chance that one of us has broken a rule, we simply remind the other. It's a pretty easy system. The other suggestion I would make is that it's important to encourage each other. For example, if I know my roommate has a test, I will leave a little encouraging note on her desk—it's a little gesture but it lets her know I care.

Jonny: I'll throw in one more tip just because it worked out so well for me: Don't be afraid to ask someone to be your roommate for the next year early. Even if you don't know the person entirely well, it's better to ask. The first time I had lunch with my current roommate, I asked him to be my roommate. It was definitely a God thing. He put someone in my life I knew I would room with well even though I barely knew him. If God wants you to room with a person next year, you will know. Once you know, don't hesitate to ask that person.

chapter 13

Crazy Things Christians Believe

We met that morning at the Taco Bell across the street from the best break at Huntington Beach. It was just shy of six a.m. and we still had sleep in our eyes, but we were stoked to be getting there so early, beating the crowds of surfers. We crossed the street and stood on the edge of the beach looking at where we'd enter the water for our weekly surf session. I was standing there with my good friends Nelson, Reed, Anthony, and a new friend of ours, John, who was becoming more known in the surfing community as one of the up-and-coming greats.

I'd first met John when a bunch of us grabbed breakfast burritos at the pier a few months earlier. Since then he and I had started to cultivate a bit of a friendship. Now something you should know about John is that he was not just an amazing surfer, he was also brilliant and was studying philosophy at Long Beach State. And he thought it was odd that someone like me would be a follower of Jesus.

So we got our gear, put on our wetsuits, and headed to the water—me a little slower than the rest of them, which is typical for a novice.

I watched as they paddled up and over the waves, just missing the breaking water and the explosion of its aftermath between us. I stood there with chills all over my body. I felt a hint of fear and excitement.

"Okay, Brock, get out there," I whispered to myself.

So I made my way out and joined them in the quiet, waiting for the first set. We sat there on our boards as the sun was rising to the east, causing the Pacific to transition from dark and ominous to a beautiful emerald green. The waiting is actually my favorite part of surfing, just sitting there in all of the beauty. I took a deep breath with my eyes closed, waiting for the first set to come rolling in, and then John paddled over to me. We sat close together on our boards with our backs to the beach.

"Brock, I still have no idea how you're a Christian," he said with a smirk.

This conversation was ongoing over the past few weeks.

"Dude, I've got my reasons," I laughed and splashed him with water. Then we heard Reed yell, "Sweet! Here they come!"

They were slow rollers with a nice gentle throw to them, which was good for me. We all jumped on the first break. I stood and rode for a few seconds before losing my balance and slipping into the ocean under the swell.

Then we all paddled out again and the waiting game began a second time. John and his questions or—more accurately—smart remarks was right beside me.

"I mean, how can you even be one of those Christians? Just to be associated with organized religion ..."

"Why do you say that?" I responded.

"Well," he said, "don't you realize all the hateful things that they have been a part of? All of the crazy things they have believed which led to them promoting slavery and violence and wars. I mean, just look at the Crusades!"

I sat there with my heart pumping, wondering what to say. Then inspiration came. "I know." I said, "I mean, there have been so many embarrassing things that Christians have done. Do you remember when that televangelist in the 80s who preached health and wealth and all about how God just wanted to make us happy? Then he got caught with that prostitute? Dude, the worst was when Jim Carrey impersonated him on that TV show *In Living Color*. I wasn't sure if I should cringe or laugh."

"Ha! I totally remember that, and I loved that show! But man, we never really heard from that guy again." He chuckled, thinking of the fallen televangelist.

"Yeah, I guess he lost his career and then his wealth and then I'm guessing his happiness." I said with a smile. "I remember when I was in fourth grade and some Christian at the time had predicted the end of the world, a doomsday sort of thing. I was going to a Christian private school at the time and our teacher brought it up. It actually kind of made me scared, and so I spent most of the day trying not to think about it all day."

"What kind of teacher would tell kids that?" John shook his head.

But I continued. "I mean, this guy was a famous Christian, and so he must be right, right?" I laughed. "Of course that day came and went and I realized there are some people who truly believe some pretty crazy things. I even heard this guy is still out there predicting the end of the world."

"But we're still here."

"I know, it just seems like too much, y'know?" I squinted at sunlight beginning to reflect off the coming waves. The swells were bigger. My heart began to pound.

"Dude, here's the next set," John said, pointing out in front.

But these were huge ten-footers coming at us. I yelled that I wasn't about to take one on, and I paddled further out into the deep before the massive waves crashed on my head. John laughed and paddled out with me, skipping the set, so our conversation continued.

He looked at me and said, "See you do get it. That's what's crazy. I don't understand how you can be a Christian when you agree with me."

I looked at him a bit puzzled and said, "I do agree with you. And yes, Christians have believed and done some pretty insane things over the years. But I think that's also true of humans in general. We've always believed, done, and participated in crazy things."

"Yeah, maybe you're right.".

"Did you know that there was a woman named Emma who had her named changed to Frank Thompson?"

"What?" John looked at me quizzically. I could tell he didn't know where this was going.

"Yeah, she was a woman who lived during the time when slavery was booming in the 1800s. She loved Jesus and because of her relationship with him, she felt compelled to join the abolition movement. "

"Really? What does that have to do with her name?" he asked.

"Well, she actually moved down to the northern states from Canada and ended up going undercover, dressing as a man to get secret information for the abolitionists. Many credited her for getting information that was key for the North. They won many battles because of it. But she did it because of her faith."

"That's crazy!"

"Or if you think of the Red Cross, the Salvation Army, Alcoholic Anonymous, even most Ivy League schools, or companies like Toms—these were all started by Christians who were overwhelmed by God's call to do something significant in the world. But I totally get what you're saying. I am ashamed at many things Christians have done in the name of God, and it breaks my heart. But the opposite is just so true as well. Go to Africa today or Haiti and meet people who are caring for the broken, the poor, the hungry, and the sick. More than likely they are quiet, humble followers of Jesus working in the ghettos and villages and trash heaps where the marginalized live." I went on, "And John, I do have intellectual and logical reasons for being a Christian, but ultimately I think I have just kind of opened my mind up to God, and he has truly shown up. I mean, look at what we're doing today, and how our group is becoming family, and we're living life together, and surrounded by all of this beauty. The sky, the ocean, and us—it's kind of miraculous. Some people in the world—maybe you included—look at us and all of creation and think it's all a big accident. I just don't see it that way, y'know?"

He looked at me in deep thought and said, "Yeah, I guess I get it. But why Jesus?"

I looked at the water. It had grown flat over the past few minutes. Each ripple shimmered in the early morning sunlight. It's the question I had been hoping he would ask for a few weeks now. Now the moment was here and of course my mind went blank. Slowly the blankness gave way to calm and a few thoughts took shape. I gathered them together and continued the conversation. "I knew there had to be a cause for all of this. Cause and effect. Someone had to do all of this. But one day I heard a guy speak about Jesus in a way that I'd never heard anyone speak before. And this guy was really cool. The way he described Jesus was in a way that seemed like Jesus was knowable, like he was his friend. And I thought, if this is true, then I want it! I want what he has. So I just opened my life to Jesus. The crazy thing is, he showed up."

John's brow furrowed. A breeze picked up and some spray dusted our faces causing us to laugh. Then he got serious again. "How? In what way?" he asked.

"Well, initially in subtle small ways. And then this might sound weird, but I was overwhelmed by a presence. I can't really explain it, but I felt supernaturally loved, accepted, and cared for. I know. I know it sounds crazy," I said.

"Actually, no." He smiled. "I went to a camp when I was in middle school, and I felt something like that. But I just kind of chalked it up to eating too much sugar and not getting enough sleep that week." He laughed.

Nelson came paddling out to us, "Guys, you're missing all of this surf!" He turned his board and straddled it, facing us. "What's going on over here?"

"Just talking about how crazy I think it is that Brock's a Christian."

We all laughed.

"I was just getting ready to tell John how I did a scientific experiment to see if Jesus was real," I said.

"Oh, good," John said. "Do tell."

"Well, like I was saying, that guy told me about Jesus, and I just decided to take all of my doubts, questions, and skepticism and put them to the side for a minute. Now I came back to those doubts, because they are an important part of having an intellectual faith. But initially I just sat them to the side and said a little prayer: 'Jesus, if you're real, then you've got to show up and work in my life. You've got to give me peace, I need that right now.' I kept praying that prayer and embraced the mystery."

Nelson spoke up and said, "Oh yeah, I heard Bono from the band U2—"

I interrupted, "Oh no, there he goes quoting Bono again!" And we all laughed.

"I know." Nelson shrugged. "I love U2, but Bono said something about how he felt it was very plausible that Jesus actually was who he said he was. And then he opened his life to God, and

Jesus has been a presence in his life ever since."

"John," I said, "Look, there are so many valid reasons not to believe in God, and I get that. I've had to wrestle with those things in major ways ever since I opened myself up to God. But ultimately we're all on a journey, and we're all smart people, and we all arrive at different places on this topic. I just hope you take your shot, y'know? Just take a shot and see if God's real."

At that we laid down and started paddling back into the break. John caught the first wave, leaving us behind. Nelson and I just sat there watching him, as the strength of the water pushed his board and shot him out the other side. Amazed at John's seemingly effortless ability, Nelson yelled, "Dude, that was sick!"

Under my breath I prayed, "God, soften his heart, reveal yourself to him. Help him to take his shot. " And then I caught my second wave of the morning.

whatever you do in life,

surround yourself

with smart people
who'll argue with you.

john wooden

chapter 14

An Intellectual Faith

I went home that night with a pit in my stomach. I had so many questions, questions that I had never really had before; this night hadn't ended the way I thought it would.

Earlier that evening I knew we were going to get into trouble. My buddy Jimmy and I were goofing off during the entire talk at youth group. We were both in tenth grade and just absolutely being ridiculous—distracting everyone, even the speaker. Afterwards the inevitable happened. Our youth pastor came up to us and asked if he could talk with us for a moment.

We stepped into the kitchen next to the gymnasium that our group met in and he began his speech, "Guys, I'm surprised at how you were acting tonight. I consider you leaders of this group. You set an example and help me minister to the other students."

Jimmy shot right back with, "Man, I don't even believe in this stuff!" And our youth pastor looked absolutely shocked. Heck, I was shocked. But Jimmy went on, "Yeah, I stopped believing all of this about a year ago and I might not even keep coming to youth group anymore."

I couldn't believe what he was saying. He'd been my friend for a couple of years now; and while we had never talked about our faith, I always thought he felt the way I did about God. I left that night wondering why he never said anything and if maybe I should be doubting as well. Did he know something I didn't?

To be honest, this little interaction shook me up a bit. At that time in my life I hadn't thought much about why I believed, what I believed, and if it was even logical or reasonable. So that evening in my sophomore year of high school I chose to start a life-long journey that has continued to this day, that has led me into deeper understanding. But initially it was pretty scary.

For me to begin the journey into questioning all things was a bit terrifying, because I wasn't sure where it would end up. I had a close relationship with my parents and they had a passionate faith in Jesus. Was this going to ruin our relationship and our bond as a family? I had to make some courageous decisions and head out into that unchartered territory. But what I came to understand is that faith without doubt is shallow, not well thought out, and extremely fragile. Asking questions was actually going to bring depth to my shallowness, thought to my faith, and would give me clarity. This was going to help prepare me to actually live out my faith in a much more profound way.

> But in your hearts revere Christ as Lord. Always be prepared to give an answer to everyone who asks you to give the reason for the hope that you have. But do this with gentleness and respect.
>
> 1 Peter 3:15

After that night when I heard Jimmy verbalize his doubts, I remember struggling myself with some deep questions. Finally I told my dad that I was beginning to have some pretty heavy uncertainty about the faith. His response was not at all what I was expecting when he said, "Good, Brock, it's important to ask questions and to seek deeper understanding. I'm proud of you!"

What? I thought. *He's proud of me?*

See, my dad and other thoughtful people in my life knew that truth was not the enemy, that we should never be afraid of truth, and we should seek it with our everything. In Matthew 22:37 the scriptures even tell us to love the Lord with all of our minds.

Many in the world think that in order to be a Christian you must leave your brain at the door of the church or that you've got to turn your intellect off and stop all rational thinking. But I wanted to know what was true, no matter where it led me, and I was reassured that this was okay. Knowing that I was part of a great tradition of thinkers going back thousands of years, who decided to love God with their entire minds was a comfort to me. I wasn't going to accept easy pat answers, but instead join those before me who used their minds and, in doing so, discovered something that sustained their faith and led them into greater discovery. So I started this journey of asking thoughtful questions at the age of fifteen.

But I wasn't alone. Maybe the biggest mistake most people make—and my friend Jimmy made—was doubting in isolation.

The church sometimes doesn't feel like a safe place to verbalize our questions, so we end up only talking with other skeptics
which can lead to a narrow perspective. I've noticed over the
years that doubt in isolation can lead to a lost faith and usually
lost faith for the wrong reasons.

Fortunately I began this journey by dialoging with as many people as I could. What it led to was a wide, thoughtful, and logical
faith.

In the summer of 2010, I took a new job at a church called Trinity in Greenwich, Connecticut, just outside of New York City.
Now let me tell you a little bit about Greenwich.

People tend to move here once they've "made it" in The Big Ap-
ple. It's a small city full of successful artists, actors, musicians,
and Wall Street money; it's also a melting pot of cultures and
worldviews. Churches sit empty all over the city as a sign that
faith is dead. Christianity isn't even a blip on the cultural screen
in most of New England.

Now, a couple of years ago I was speaking at an amazing youth
camp in Michigan, and I met the worship band that had been
brought in for the weekend from Canada. They tour all over the
United States and are fairly successful. When they learned that
I was a youth pastor in New England, they were amazed. They
don't even attempt to play the Northeast, they just drive on home
to Canada. There is no place for a Christian worship band here.

In Greenwich, many public school students take a class that
scoffs at biblical stories, reducing them down to fairytales. It's
a class that basically breeds agnostic thinking. The gist of it is
that any intelligent person could never hold to such things, nor

should they investigate further. Students in my youth group have grown up surrounded by liberal reductionism, and the church has no voice in the community's mindset.

In fact a student recently told me that he couldn't be a Christian because of science. Inside I thought, "Wow, science has actually helped my faith!"

I love C. S. Lewis's book, *Mere Christianity*. In it he writes, "Ever since people were able to think, they have been wondering what this universe really is and how it came to be there."

Since the dawn of time we have been asking the great questions of why and how and who. We want to know, but for some reason many Christians over the millennia have tried to stop the questions. Maybe it's fear, maybe it's control, or maybe it's insecurity or a mixture of them all. But many young emerging adults feel they have to leave the faith just because they have these burning and very natural questions. They feel like they can't stay in order to ask the big questions.

At my youth group in California we would have quarterly "doubt nights." These were my favorite nights of the year. Students would write down their questions and their doubts the week before, then the following week we'd read them aloud and affirm them. Many would be humbly answered, but when it came to others we'd just appreciate the depth of the question and sit with it and soak in the mystery of it. The great thing is that our youth group, through those times, realized that questions were normal. They were natural and they were critical to actually having a vibrant, real faith. You have to ask questions. In fact, as Christians we have to keep these big questions alive because they forge pathways into a deeper faith that is stable yet full of mystery.
The cool thing is that we would end every "doubt night" in exuberant worship. I have never seen students worship with such

passion as on those nights. Kids realized how big God was, that he could handle our questions, and our questions revealed how mighty he really was. That he was and is beyond us.

But again questioning is not always looked at fondly in religious circles. Most recently this idea started during the nineteenth century when liberalism began its rise and Darwinism was gaining steam. Because of the church's poor response to Darwin's theories about evolution, science was now on the offense, and Christianity was left to play defense.

Instead of embracing science, Christians defended their position and insulated themselves against the world. They appeared angry, unintelligent, and backward to those on the outside. Instead of joining the conversation and seeking truth, they turned inward, preached to the choir, and lost their voices in the world.

At one time Christianity was known for its leaders in philosophy, in education, and for creatively engaging the culture around them. But now many Christians see culture as the enemy. We turned against culture and taught our children how to defend their faith instead of simply living it out in the world. And this change in our position created the "us versus them" construct. I don't blame Christians for responding the way they did. It was a scary time. I get it. But the result is that young adults today feel like they're not allowed to seek truth and ask questions.

Another great example of this was in the year 1633, when the church found the scientist Galileo guilty of heresy because he wrote and taught that the earth revolved around the sun rather than the other way around. Yes, that really happened, and the church's flawed reasoning for rejecting science was based on a handful of vague verses whose main points were arguably not the rotation of heavenly bodies. See, Christians have, at times, gotten into trouble because they used Scripture in the wrong way, interpreted the Bible the wrong way, and stifled our God-given ability to explore scientific truth.

See, God wants us to use our minds, and he's not afraid of where that might lead us.

The brilliant director of the National Institutes of Health (NIH), Dr. Francis Collins, is credited with mapping the human genome. And he's also a follower of Jesus. He used his intellect, and it led him not only to the Big Bang, but to a life dedicated to following Jesus. Yes, Christians can be theistic evolutionists. In his book *The Language of God* (Free Press, 2007), Collins said this:

> We have this very solid conclusion that the universe had an origin, the Big Bang. Fifteen billion years ago, the universe began with an unimaginably bright flash of energy from an infinitesimally small point. That implies that before that, there was nothing. I can't imagine how nature, in this case the universe, could have created itself. And the very fact that the universe had a beginning implies that someone was able to begin it. And it seems to me that had to be outside of nature. And that sounds like God.

My father-in-law is a brilliant scientist and a pre-med professor. His studies led him to believe in a literal six-day creation. And that's okay too. His students become doctors, nurses, and researchers who love God, love people, and do excellent work. See, there is room enough in the faith for my father in-law, Francis Collins, you, and even me. We can humbly bring up our questions and follow truth wherever it leads us.

Collins goes on to say in *The Language of God*:

> I do not believe that the God who created all the uni-

verse, and who communes with his people through prayer and spiritual insight, would expect us to deny the obvious truths of the natural world that science has revealed to us, in order to prove our love for him.

I actually think my father-in-law and Dr. Collins would get along famously. The point and the biggest question might in fact be this: Who made us ask these questions anyway? Is it a clue that God wants us to lean into the questions? Because maybe the question of why will eventually lead us to God.

I love hearing scientists talk about how the cosmos points to a reality that there's design and order to the universe; that a belief in God is a very logical thing. I like how Francis Collins describes it:

> When you look from the perspective of a scientist at the universe, it looks as if it knew we were coming. There are fifteen constants—the gravitational constant, various constants about the strong and weak nuclear force, etc.—that have precise values. If any one of those constants was off by even one part in a million, or in some cases, by one part in a million million, the universe could not have actually come to the point where we see it. Matter would not have been able to coalesce, there would have been no galaxy, stars, planets or people.

In the documentary *Stephen Hawking's Universe* (PBS, 1997), even Hawking—a self-proclaimed atheist—admits, "The odds against a universe like ours emerging out of something like the Big Bang are enormous. I think there are clearly religious implications." He goes on to say: "It would be very difficult to explain why the universe would have begun in just this way except as the act of a God who intended to create beings like us."

Yet Hawking still holds to his atheistic faith, all the while admitting it is fragile. Even Plato decided that it was reasonable to believe in God based on "the order of the motion of the stars, and of all things under the dominion of the mind which ordered the universe" (from Plato's *Laws*).

Every summer I look forward to camp. To getting away from the noise of life and getting away from all the light pollution, heading out to where the stars shine so bright you feel like you could reach up and touch them. On those clear camp nights I love sitting with students in the quiet, just gazing upon the beauty of the sky and all of its fullness. Sir Isaac Newton said: "When I look at the solar system, I see the earth at the right distance from the sun to receive the proper amounts of heat and light. This did not happen by chance" (*Isaac Newton* by John Hudson Tiner; Mott Media, 1975). On those nights under the stars, I love hearing students talk about how creation is pointing them to a creator.

GOD wants us to use **our minds**,
and he's not afraid of where that might lead us.

Ben Valentine, our church's high school pastor, was teaching through some of these principles to our students and taught, "Every design reflects its designer. Chart the path of the stars, measure the rate of decay in an atom, examine the laws of physics, everything you study is well-ordered, precise, and complex." Albert Einstein agrees, and he's quoted as saying, "The mathematical precision of the universe reveals the mathematical mind of God."

See, I've got questions—some that I can't wait to ask God myself when I see him face to face; but I'll say this, truth has been leading me to him ever since I was fifteen. In the words of C. S. Lewis in *Mere Christianity*:

> God is no fonder of intellectual slackers than of any other slackers. If you are thinking of becoming a Christian, I warn you, you are embarking on something which is going to take the whole of you, brains and all.

We want to have the whole of us, brains and all, on this journey.

chapter 15

My (Pretend) Conversation with N. T. Wright*

I've been a major fan of N. T. (Tom) Wright for many years now. I like to think I was a fan before anyone else had heard of him, but that's just my humble assertion. He's a well-respected historian who is a Bible scholar and a best-selling author. He's been featured on *ABC News*, *Dateline*, and *The Colbert Report*—just to name a few. Plus he's British, so even when he orders a cup of black coffee, it sounds brilliant. I actually have spoken to him briefly, but because of time and circumstances our exchange was nothing to write home about.

So, I've decided to have a pretend conversation with him instead, and I think you'll agree … Tom's a pretty cool guy.

*The conversation detailed here did not actually occur—hence the word pretend—but is instead an awesome figment of my imagination fueled by the reading of Tom's many theological works, particularly *Surprised by Scripture* (HarperCollins, 2014).

Brock: So, Tom, I understand you've read my book, *Youth Ministry in a Post-Christian World*. What were your thoughts?

Tom: Well I must say, your writing is ground-breaking and brilliant, just absolutely brilliant!

Brock: I'm so honored to hear you say that, Tom. I really am. I mean, you don't know what it means to hear you—well, I mean, okay. I suppose we should just get to the point. I really want to ask you about the resurrection of Jesus. This is a big feature of the stories we find in the Gospels. Do we really need a resurrection?

Tom: Well, Brock, I wrote about this in various places, but most recently in my book, *Surprised by Scripture*—published by HarperCollins and available at a bookstore near you—so let me just quickly summarize a few points in there. As you know, Paul the Apostle believed that if we don't have a resurrected Jesus, then all we have is a dead rabbi. The Christian claim from the beginning was that Jesus' resurrection was something that actually happened in the real world, in actual time. And he left with us evidence, namely an empty tomb, a broken loaf of bread after eating with disciples, footprints in the sand by the lake, and so much more. For the early church followers, the evidence was overwhelming, and they all believed that something physical actually happened. His followers, as a result, wound up with a completely transformed worldview. For them, everything changed because of the resurrection of Jesus. They saw him and truly believed that what they were experiencing firsthand was real and true. Unlike this conversa—

Brock: Ahem. Sorry. Something in my throat, I guess. So can you talk more about the evidence that Jesus did leave us and what kind of evidence would lead the early followers of Jesus to truly believe in such a thing?

Tom: There is so much to say but let me begin with this: The early Christians came from a massively diverse group. That may not sound like a big deal for those of us who live in a diverse world. But in the Middle East at that time, this was significant! The resurrection of Jesus brought people together who never would've even interacted let alone become family. They didn't just come from many different strands of Judaism but also from widely differing backgrounds within all kinds of paganism.

All of these different people with their respective religions and differing deity perspectives and worldviews landed on the exact same conclusion. They came in with different belief systems from each other only to have them radically altered all because of this one event that they really believed happened. And these were no idiots. They knew that dead people stayed dead. This was an anomaly. This was life-altering in the most significant ways possible.

Brock: I do find that very interesting since my own family, with our shared culture and point of view, can hardly agree on what the movie *Interstellar* is even about. But what else?

Tom: So, the miracle of the resurrection brought people together, but the second thing I'd mention is that without it, you basically have nothing. Zero plus zero will always equal zero. Without the resurrection, nothing would have happened. In other words you can't imagine the disciples doing anything at all. You can't imagine Paul the Apostle's work without it. You couldn't imagine John's teaching without it. Take away the stories of Jesus' birth, and all you lose is four chapters of the Gospels. Take away the resurrection and you lose the entire New Testament, and most of the second-century fathers as well. Understanding the resurrection is the most important thing we can do.

The third major impact of the resurrection would be this: The

Jews had an understanding of the resurrection that was significantly altered as well. Every Jew, prior to the resurrection, believed that the prophesied resurrection would be a large-scale event happening to God's people or perhaps to the entire human race at the very end of time. Not in the middle of history. This just was not a part of the Jewish teaching. But this belief in resurrection, because of Jesus, becomes a central feature within the early church movement. And these believers had their past belief about the prophesied resurrection altered—they now believed that what happened with Jesus was a foreshadowing, an exact parallel of what would happened to all of humanity at the end of history. It clarified a teaching—a prophecy—that had not been clear before.

Brock: So, Jesus' resurrection is a picture of what will happen to each of us one day?

Tom: Yes, precisely. And that leads us to my next point. The fifth impact of the resurrection is that the early church believed that the resurrection had begun with Jesus and would be completed in the great final resurrection on the last day. These followers of Jesus saw themselves as co-collaborators with God and really believed that they were called to put into effect Jesus' achievement in the present time.

Brock: Oh, I like this. Explain more.

Tom: See, Jesus had overcome death. What these Jesus followers anticipated was that the same would happen to them—that they too would be transformed—but until that would happen they would be charged with bringing change and transformation and goodness to the world in which they currently lived. Those who belonged to Jesus and followed him in the power of his spirit were charged with transforming the present, as far as they were able, in light of that future.

Brock: Now that is huge. I never really connected the resurrection with our mission to bring God's future into the present, to be his light and final hope in this moment, here and now. That's amazing!

Tom: Another thing about the resurrection—number six, if you're keeping count—that's so important is that no Jew believed that their Messiah would ever die. So, of course, no one would believe that there would ever even be the need for their Messiah to be resurrected. This leads us to the remarkable change in belief concerning the Messiah. The Messiah was supposed to come and fight against God's enemies and free the world of paganism. He would rebuild the temple and cleanse it, and bring God's justice from one end of the world to the other. But Jesus did none of these things. No Jew with any understanding of the language used about the Messiah could have possibly imagined, after the crucifixion, that Jesus of Nazareth was indeed the Lord's anointed. But from the beginning Christians affirmed that Jesus was indeed the Messiah precisely because of the resurrection. The belief in Jesus as Messiah makes little sense without the resurrection.

You have to know that this was not at all unusual for someone to claim to be the Messiah. There were many Jewish movements who claimed their leader as the Messiah. But each time the Roman army or a Jewish enemy would come and kill the would-be Messiah, their movement would end. You can't follow a dead Messiah, because that Messiah was supposed to rid the world of their enemies. Routinely these claims of messianic authority ended with the violent death of the central figure. Members of the movements then had a significant choice to make: either give up the struggle because our leader has been killed or find a new leader. The disciples could have made one of these two common choices. They had others that could have easily stepped up and become the leader of this movement if they truly wanted it to continue. James, the Lord's brother would have been the perfect choice. He was a central figure in the early church movement. But nobody ever imagined that James might be the Messiah. Why? Because they saw the risen Jesus.

Brock: Alright, I really want the reader to catch this, because this is really important for us. Can you explain further this idea of other movements that ended with the death of their messiah?

Tom: Sure. Let's act like we have a time machine and let's go back to Rome in AD 70 and let's watch the flogging and execution of Simon bar Giora. He was called, by his followers, the "King of the Jews." Now let's imagine that we overhear a few Jewish revolutionaries three days later talking.

The first revolutionary says, "I know for a fact that Simon really was the Messiah!"

The others would be confused and think he was ridiculous. They'd say, "No way! He's definitely not the Messiah—Rome killed him so you better just go and find yourself a new Messiah."

"No," says the first, "but I really believe that he is actually alive and risen from the dead."

"What are you saying?" his friends ask. "He's in a grave, man!"

"Oh, no," replies the first, "I believe he's in heaven and he's been glorified there."

The others look confused, baffled even. "All the holy martyrs are in heaven and they're with God; everyone already knows this. We all know that a true martyr for God's kingdom is in God's presence. That doesn't mean that they've been raised from the dead! Plus, we know that at the end of time the resurrection will happen to all of humanity."

"You guys just don't get it," replies the first, "I know this to be true because I've been overwhelmed by God's presence and by his love. I've felt God working in me and I have this strong sense that God has forgiven me—he's forgiving us all. I sense that I have been changed. And also, last night I saw Simon—he visited me!"

The others stop him and interrupt, now angry. "Everyone and anyone can have a vision now and again. People do this all of the time. We all have dreams. But that does not mean that Simon was raised from the dead. He's not the Messiah! And if you feel God's presence, then sing a song of praise, but don't make a ridiculous claim."

Now you can imagine if only one of Jesus' disciples claimed this, he would have had this kind of conversation again and again. His belief would have been deemed a vision, a confused and maybe well-meaning hope in a hopeless cause.

Brock: Yes, but many saw the risen Jesus, not just one person. And many died for this belief, were tortured for this belief. They really believed it, even when their lives were at stake. Then you take into account the prophecies that actually came true in the crucifixion and resurrection and what you have is very real and profound evidence for us to investigate.

Now, Tom, this has been amazing but I know we are just scratching the surface. I'd love anyone who is reading this to pick up your book, *Surprised by Scripture*—published by HarperCollins and available at a bookstore near you—and read it. The educated and logical reasoning is amazing. Thank you, Tom, for your work that is advancing the kingdom and awakening our minds.

Tom: Well thank you, Brock, and thanks again for your brilliant work. I'm a huge fan.

Brock: Wow, man. I mean, I couldn't think of a better note for us to end on. This is just how I always pictured it …

chapter 16

Group Chat | Can Faith Thrive in the College Years?

Many students wonder about going away to college and keeping their faith. They might even wonder if they've got a faith worth keeping. I've gathered a few college students—Evan, Troone, Zoe, Jonny, Heather, Casey, and Krista—who are on this rollercoaster ride of a journey themselves. I've asked them to talk about faith and these transformative years, and I hope their conversation is helpful to you.

How can someone grow their faith in college? We hear a lot about students losing their faith or seeing the faith become stagnant in college. How does some one go away to college and thrive?

Heather: First I'd say it's vital to find a church you connect with. For my first couple months in college I participated in an internship working with a youth group at this local church near my college. I really enjoyed working with the kids; they were terrific! Smart, curious, and truly wanted to know God. The only problem with the internship was that it required me to attend a certain church on the weekends, and although I tried to connect with the church, I never walked out of the service feeling fulfilled. At home, I loved my church—the worship consisted of a full-fledged band and contemporary Christian music and the sermons were always engaging, intelligent, and inspiring. And the people I met there were incredible too. Although this church (the one connected to my internship) may have helped some to connect with God, I was personally not gaining anything from attending the services.

One day my friend invited me to come and see her church, since she knew I wasn't happy at the one I was attending. So I joined her and immediately felt at home at this new church. I spoke with my internship advisor and now attend church with my friend every Sunday. I realized that spending time in comfortable community and connecting with God weekly was more important than attending a church out of obligation. I only wish I had found this church sooner.

Casey: Yes! Don't wait until second semester. Also, make it a commitment to go, don't be flaky. Make church a part of your schedule. Act as if it is a three or four credit mandatory class. Having like-minded friends who are going to lift you up and cause you to grow closer to God and not be affected by the college social scene is key. I believe 1 Corinthians 15:33 isn't kidding when it talks about bad company corrupting good morals … trust me. With a steady church you are bound to find people who are going to encourage excellence in your life.

Troone: Finding a church can be really hard though, especially if you've been at the same church your whole life, or have never "church hunted" before. It's especially hard the first weeks of school because so many things are fighting for your attention, and you may not feel like waking up early on a Sunday morning, tired, and possibly hung over, to go to a church service you haven't been to before, where you probably don't know anyone. It pays off though. It pays off, and when you do find the church community that's right for you, it can be transformative, like it was for me. This past semester, I would want to go out with my friends on Saturday night, and then wake up at 8:30 a.m. to be at my 10:30 church service—a journey which took exactly eighty-five minutes every Sunday morning. Broken up into three parts too—a thirty-five-minute walk, thirty-minute bus ride, and another twenty-minute walk.

At the beginning of the semester I would go out to parties on Saturday nights with my friends, then wake up after a few hours of sleep and drag myself to church. But after a few weeks I realized I wasn't getting everything I wanted out of church. I was getting there exhausted, couldn't have the deep conversations I wanted to be able to have, and felt embarrassed by the dark circles that I knew surrounded my eyes. So I decided I was going to stop going out and partying on Saturday nights.

This changed so much of my life. It meant I was able to pour more into my Christian friendships and dig deeper. I was getting more out of worship and sermons and began to transform not only the person I was on Sundays, but the person I was the other six days of the week.

For college students, your time is your currency. There's only one-hundred and sixty-eight hours in a week. Some of those will go toward sleep, some toward going to class, some to studying, some to eating. But the others make up your "free time." That's when you get to choose what club meetings you go to, which friends you hang out with, what parties you go to. These are the things that shape you and the person you become. If you're putting all your free time into partying and then you sleep until two in the afternoon the next day and then have to do all your studying, you will not be feeding your spiritual life.

Evan: Yes, you've got to find a good church—that's really important. Somewhere with worship and sermons that you like. And finding a community is everything—somewhere with a small group of other college students that you can meet with in a small group or Bible study or even just to hang out with regularly. This doesn't necessarily have to be the same church. It's just so important to find your faith for yourself and hold yourself accountable—you're off on your own, so for those people who have had their parents bring them to church their whole lives, now is the time to really discover your own love for Jesus. After all, it's only worth going if you really want to go.

I also found that I needed to just commit. There will always be work, studying, hanging out, or other events that can seem more pressing or important than a small group meeting or church once a week, but these things will always be there. Committing yourself to going can make a difference, and the peace you get can actually help you to do homework or whatever else you need to do

I'd also say that it is important to explore—especially if you haven't that much. Push yourself to examine and critique your own views. Doubt yourself, because that's the easiest way to develop and solidify your faith. Don't just believe it because your parents do, because you were raised to, because it's easier, or because it "kind of makes sense." Studying arguments against Christianity has actually helped strengthen my faith so much.

Krista: For me it has actually been easier to keep my faith alive in college. I made a decision from the very beginning that my faith had to be the biggest and greatest part of my life. I thought, "If this is the most vital part of my life, then why would I waste my time trying to find something else?" So, I surrounded myself with people that would feed my faith rather than drain it. I know it's been said, but I think the biggest thing is finding a community or a church that you love—people who will be your family and keep you accountable.

Heather: Yes, I agree with Krista about finding friends who love Jesus and who will walk with you in your faith journey. I can say with absolute confidence that the friends I have met in the first six months of college will be my friends for life, simply because I can share and talk to them about my faith. When I have questions or am feeling angry or sad, I can talk to these friends. Like my youth group in high school, they love me unconditionally and not only affirm my faith, but also encourage me in it.

For example, my friends and I have a group chat in which we post prayer requests and also inspiring verses of the week. I also constantly pray with my friends and attend church with them. We also give each other reading suggestions to help grow our faith. This is not to say we are by any means perfect. We are about as crazy and stupid as they come. With these same friends we take late-night drives to Chick-fil-A and Chipotle, we have stargazing sessions at two a.m. because we can; we go to the beach and surf together; we have late night study sessions together … what I'm trying to say is that it's important to surround yourself with friends you feel comfortable with and who you can do crazy things with, but also people who love you and love Jesus.

Troone: Having Christian friends means you don't feel like you're alone when you choose not to go out on Saturday night so you can be awake for church the next morning. You can still have a good time and not be wasted or feel left out when you're opening all of your non-Christian friends' Snapchat stories. To have people around you who you know are facing the same temptations at college and are saying no, binds you together and helps you take much bigger steps in your faith than you'd be able to take alone.

Jonny: We really need to live with a hunger—where we really want to know the Lord. So inviting people into that to help you grow in your faith is so important. The bottom line is that it is quite essential to get rid of this fear and ask people for help. God has put other brothers and sisters in Christ in your life for a reason, and that reason is to help you grow in your faith.

Zoe: For me, I think the hardest thing about starting college is that there are too many things you're going to want to do, and realistically you're not going to be able to do it all. The things that truly fill you up will too easily get swept away in the busyness and craziness of trying to do everything new and exciting in college. Finding a community of people who can inspire and encourage you to go deeper in your faith is essential to keeping your faith alive in college. It may sound simple, but it's much more difficult than you would think. Don't waste a Sunday. Immediately start pursuing Jesus in the places where his spirit can be felt from the moment you step through the doors. Continuing your relationship with God should be one of your first priorities in college. If it's not, it will slowly float to the background along with everything else that didn't get top priority.

Troone: When you arrive at college your first week, you're hit with everything: saying goodbye to your parents, living with a stranger, constantly meeting new people, and being bombarded by friend requests on Facebook, and then you get to the activity fair. I remember walking through it, looking at the faces of the people and watching their mouths move but having no idea what they were saying because of how loud it was in that room and the fact that there were fifteen other people talking to me at the same time about their own clubs.

When you get there your first week, there WILL be more things than you can keep up with competing for your attention. Therefore, going into that time it's super helpful to do a little bit of work beforehand and look online to narrow your search of communities you'd want to be a part of to make everything less intimidating. Even doing this just for Christian communities is super helpful, finding the one that's right for you. It's so important to have a Christian community while at school to lovingly hold you accountable, mentor you, and lift you up.

What about the rest of the week? Outside of just Sunday. What helps you stay spiritually aware?

Jonny: For me, daily time spent in the Word has been key. It doesn't even need to be too long of a devotional. In fact, you can have devotionals of only a few verses. What's more important is meditating on God's Word throughout the day. Have variety in the way to you read! Sometimes, read through a book of the Bible at a time. Sometimes, focus of different themes in the Bible, such as the parables of Jesus.

In addition, focus on prayer. It's so important. This is where we are developing our personal relationship with God. Prayer also reminds us how little control we have and that God is ultimately in control in every part of our life. Surrender to him and let him take control!

Troone: This past semester I had my quiet time every Monday, Wednesday, and Thursday between the end of my 10:30 class and the beginning of my 1:30 class. I would grab a coffee from Dunkin' Doughnuts and go for a walk to a quiet quad in the corner of campus, find a chair outside, listen to worship music, read the Bible and journal. This time became my daily time with

Jesus, where I could break away from the stress going on around me, break away from feeling the pressures of school and "the future" and just be. Just "being" is one important thing for life that is not taught enough in college. We're not taught to sit and embrace exactly what's around us. But when we do, that time ends up being extraordinarily fulfilling, energy-giving, and fills me with joy.

And then, be mentored. Whether it's by an adult in your church at home, your church at college, or someone at school a few grades above you or a bit farther along in their faith walk, this is something that can be life-changing during the college years. We were never meant to walk alone, and we have so much to learn from each other through sharing and mentorship. Mentors act as our "bigs"—the person you can call after you know you made a not-so-great decision last Friday night, when you need encouragement when facing temptations, or when you're feeling distant or alone. To have someone who has gone through similar circumstances share their story with you and who can support you is invaluable.

Heather: Take time alone with Jesus—this looks a little different for everyone. For me it is taking one hour from my week and sitting outside starring at the ocean, listening to worship music, and writing in my prayer journal. For my other friend this means taking five minutes every morning to read a Bible verse and pray. In any case, although God did make us to live in community with others it's important to spend time alone, listening for how he wants to speak into your life. I've found as the semester gets busier and busier this becomes harder and harder to do. Your schoolwork becomes harder and more abundant, your social calendar becomes full, and you are pretty much running on coffee, never mind sleep. Still ... take the time—whether it's five minutes or an hour—to just sit with God and listen. Often he has surprised me, and I always come away feeling refreshed and ready to take on the world.

Evan: I did this sort of "life experiment" for two weeks during my freshman year to try to focus every part of my life on Jesus. Every time I looked at the time and it was a new hour, I would say a prayer. Just to talk to Jesus—casually, as if he were a good friend. Whatever was on my mind, all of the things I could think of at the time that I was thankful were going right—a list I quickly discovered was quite infinite. What I found was that even on my worst days—when there were maybe four or five things I could point out that went wrong—still, every single day I could sit down and pray for hours and hours thanking God for things that went right. I found myself praying to God and thanking him between classes, silently at meals, and pretty much all throughout the day. It brought me really close to God. Constantly turning my attention towards Jesus prevented me from losing patience and making irrational decisions—ultimately leading to the most peaceful two weeks of my life.

true **freedom**
is impossible without a mind
made free by **discipline**.
mortimer j. adler

chapter 17

Red Solo Cup

"Brock, did you see April's Instagram pictures?"

"No. Why?"

"Well. *You* know ... she's holding a red cup."

"Oh ..."

Red cups never really meant anything a few years ago. But now it's a new world. College students who don't want their parents to know they're partying can just pull out a red cup and drink anything they want without worrying about someone taking pictures and posting them where their parents might see. But a word of warning: Word is out on the red cups these days; it might be time to switch to the color blue.

I remember seeing my uncle drunk, he was about ten years older than me. I was eight years old at the time and I will never forget the feeling I felt. He was my hero; I wanted to be just like him— at least until that day. For some of us, we see something like that and it draws us in, for me it did the opposite. I saw what it was doing to him, and I made a decision to not go down that path. That didn't mean I was never going to drink, but it did mean I was going to make better choices. I wanted to live a life full of wisdom. I wanted to make thoughtful, smart decisions. I want the same for you.

I remember a high school girl telling me that she wanted to go to parties to prove that she loved God. She went on to tell me that if she was around a bunch of really tempting things and said no, then she could show God how committed she was to him. My thought was, "What, are you crazy?" Of course I didn't say that, at least, not exactly those words. But to me it just made no sense. I mean, I've never shown my wife how faithful I am by going to strip clubs and not getting a lap dance. No, I show my love to her by not going there at all.

Many people don't realize how powerful our sin nature really is. I know that I'm capable of much sin. I know that—if in the right circumstances (or wrong)—I am capable of horrid things. That's why I never tried cocaine; I knew I'd like it. I really have to guard myself against temptation.

But before we get to some things that I hope will help you navigate the party scene, I'd love to help you think about something: Many people feel like unless they're drinking, smoking, or whatever, then they're really not having fun. Please don't fall into this. I want to challenge you to help redefine what fun truly is. I personally hated seeing my friends throwing up and doing things that they regretted. I myself wanted to guard my heart and not set myself up for failure. I didn't think so highly of myself that I thought surrounding myself with temptation was a good idea.

But I do want to help give a bit of wisdom for the party scene in case you find yourself there. So here we go ...

1. Don't go alone. The last thing you want to be is alone at a party. It's not only awkward but there is also no one watching your back. You always need a wingman or woman, someone who has your best interests in mind.

2. Know your limit. I have many friends—and I made this choice as well—who chose not to drink until they were twenty-one. I highly recommend this. I mean, it is the law. But even if you're of age it's important to know the line of intoxication. For example, I know that I can't drink more than two glasses of wine. If I drink more than that I start to get a headache, and I don't feel quite right. There actually is biblical precedence for this knowing your limit thing. The scriptures tell us not to get drunk (I interpret that as high as well) in Ephesians 5.

3. Don't wander into a random person's room.
Sometimes it's nice to get away from the noise and the craziness at a college party. But you need to guard your heart and not set yourself up for a major mistake. This is another reason to have someone there with you watching your back. Awful things can happen at some of these parties. Please be smart, look out for yourself, and for others too.

4. Don't give out your number.
This one seems obvious, but it's an important one. Honestly, a party just might be the worst place to meet someone to potential-

ly date. You deserve to be in a relationship with someone who is longing to live on mission as well. Plus you don't want some moron texting you constantly. Not every person is worthy of your digits.

5. Always have a designated driver or walker.
Just in case mistakes are made, someone needs to make sure that everyone gets home safely by the end of the night.

6. Don't ever accept a drink from a stranger—male or female—even if they're cute.
The research on this one is mind-blowing, and the stories I have heard over the years of girls (in particular) getting drugged at a party are horrifying. Please be in control of everything, including what you put in your body.

7. Be aware of the stats and know you aren't immune.

Here are a few to know:
The younger you are when you start drinking, the greater your chance of becoming addicted to alcohol at some point in your life. More than four in ten people who begin drinking before age fifteen eventually become alcoholics. That's huge!

Your brain is still developing throughout the teen years and into your twenties. New research on teens with alcohol disorders shows that heavy drinking in the teen years can cause long-lasting harm to thinking abilities.

Each year, an estimated 5,000 people under the age of twenty-one die from alcohol-related injuries. Alcohol is a factor in about four of every ten deaths from car crashes, drownings, burns, falls, and other unintentional injuries.

SOURCE: http://www.thecoolspot.gov/too_much.asp

In case those aren't enough, here are some more:
Alcoholism costs the United States more each year than either cancer or obesity.

Heavy drinking can cause pancreatitis, which can be deadly.

Alcoholism and alcohol abuse increases the risk for certain cancers, from liver to colon to breast and on and on it goes.

Excessive drinking can also cause immune system problems and brain damage, not to mention permanent liver damage.

More than four in every ten American adults have a spouse, parent, sibling, or child who is an active or recovering alcoholic.

Three times as many men (9.8 million) as women (3.9 million) in the U.S. abuse alcohol or are alcohol dependent.

Growing up with an absentee father places both young women and men at a higher risk of drug and alcohol addiction.

Approximately 14 million people in the U.S. are addicted to alcohol or abuse alcohol.

Alcohol abuse and addiction are present in more than seven percent of the U.S. population, ages eighteen and older.

While alcoholism typically develops over a span of fifteen years, it happens much faster in adolescents and young adults.

One in five alcoholics who try to quit drinking on their own without proper medical supervision die of alcohol withdrawal delirium. Addiction treatment facilities are crucial to survival.

Children of alcoholics are at greater risk of becoming alcoholics themselves.

Half a million Americans dependent on alcohol are not even teenagers yet.

SOURCE: http://alcoholism-information.com/Alcoholism_ Statistics.html

often, it's not about
becoming a new person,
but becoming the person
you were meant to be,
and **already are**,
but don't know how to be.
heath l. buckmaster
box of hair: a fairy tale

chapter 18

Pass Me the Milk

Most of my life has been marked by ridiculous mistakes, imma-ture reactions, and childish decisions. Even after I got married and was a pastor, I found that my juvenile ways would occasion-ally surface at the most inopportune times.

Like the time when I was asked to come and speak at a local Christian high school. The topic they wanted me to speak on was "personal responsibility." Like I was saying, personal re-sponsibility hasn't always been my strong suit. So, my wife and I headed out to this school that I'd never been to with directions written on a napkin by a fifteen-year-old student. Needless to say, we got lost.

With about ten minutes left until I was supposed to speak and knowing we were still a good twenty minutes away, I started to speed. I remember my wife saying, "Brock, if you get a ticket, I am going to kill you!" My response was, "Baby, we're fine. There's no way I'll get a ticket." No sooner had the words left my mouth then, to my horror, flashing lights were in the rearview mirror and a siren was blasting behind my car. We pulled over and the police officer walked up to my wife's side of the car, so she rolled down her window. He pointed at me and said, "Get out of the car, buddy. You're going to jail. We've been chasing you for ten minutes on both sides of the freeway, and you're in big trouble."

My wife started crying, and not just little tears. She was balling her eyes out—and furious to boot. I got out of the car and the officer reached for his handcuffs. In a shaky voice I said, "Sir, please don't arrest me. I'm a youth pastor and I'm supposed to speak at a Christian school down the road on personal responsibility. Please don't take me to jail. Please."

God was with me that day, my friends. The officer paused for a second, put his cuffs away, and said, "Get back in your car." My wife blew her nose and, justifiably, slugged me right in the gut. The officer wrote me a ticket and gave me directions to the school. I walked into the assembly, still shaking, as the worship band finished their last song. I got on the stage and talked about the importance of being personally responsible—with a great illustration, I might add. (Oh, the irony.)

You might be thinking, "Brock, you're an idiot!" And my response to that would be, "Yep." Honestly, I have always tended to do things that I don't even want to do. Paul the Apostle shares a similar experience with the church in Rome:

For I do not do the good I want to do, but the evil I
do not want to do—this I keep on doing.

Romans 7:19

I read this and I feel a little better about myself, especially knowing that Paul can relate. But I have to tell you something, I hate
this about myself. I hate that I keep making similar mistakes over
and over again. I hate that I can't seem to get it right. I long to
become something greater, and I've always felt this way.

When I was a freshman in high school I tried out for the freshman team but was asked to play varsity. It was such an honor,
and I couldn't believe that I would letter my freshman year. So I
went to order my letterman's jacket, but I wasn't sure what size
to get. I was just a freshman with skinny arms and chicken-like
legs. My friends told me to order a large, that I'd eventually grow
into it. I believed them, since my dad is a tall, barrel-chested
man. Surely I would grow to look like him, right? So that's what
I did, I ordered a jacket that was way too big for me thinking that
I would eventually grow into it.

Problem was, I never did. I had this beautiful letterman's jacket
that was the size my father would wear. It hung off my shoulders
and swallowed up my skinny body. It was so obvious I couldn't
fill it out. And it's funny, I never did grow as much as I wanted
to. I actually ended up giving the jacket to a Goodwill in Los
Angeles. Five years later in a Starbucks twenty miles away from
the Goodwill, I ran into a homeless man wearing my letterman's
jacket. It fit him perfectly, and I got a picture with him.

My letterman jacket represents a recurring fear I have: That I
will never be "enough" spiritually. That somehow I will never
become all that I was meant to be. I fear it will be so obvious that

I'm falling short of my faith, my calling, my relationship with God. But I deeply desire to grow. So what if I never do?

Recently I was thinking of my wedding day. It was absolutely perfect. Honestly, I couldn't have been happier. I was marrying the girl of my dreams, and I knew how blessed I was. I still feel like I won the lottery with her. But I remember getting in the car after the reception to head out on our honeymoon. I held her hand and looked her in the eyes and said that she could count on one thing from me: That I would never stop growing, that I would never stop working on myself, and that I would always be striving to become better. It's been about twenty years since that day, and I can honestly say I've tried my hardest to live up to those words. I want to love her well, treat her with kindness, and be the best man I can be. But with someone like me it has taken a lot of work.

There's this amazing passage in Hebrews where Paul looks at the Hebrew people and he challenges them to move into maturity.

He says it this way in *The Message Bible*:

> By this time you ought to be teachers yourselves, yet here I find you need someone to sit down with you and go over the basics on God again, starting from square one—baby's milk, when you should have been on solid food long ago! Milk is for beginners, inexperienced in God's ways; solid food is for the mature, who have some practice in telling right from wrong. So come on, let's leave the preschool finger-painting exercises on Christ and get on with the grand work of art. Grow up in Christ.
>
> Hebrews 5:1b-6:1

I love how he puts it: "Get on with the grand work of art." That's what I long for.

At some point during my time at college, I became tired of the game. I was tired of playing church and acting like a follower of Jesus only to go out and run in the opposite direction like a child trying to escape his parent's grip at a toy store. I was tired of finger-painting silly pictures of Jesus. I actually wanted to know Jesus. In fact, I was tired of having isolated experiences with God, I wanted to live with him and actually follow him into adventure. One day I just thought: *That's it! I'm tired of the charade. God, I'm in!*

But the truth is that for so long until that point I'd been okay with spiritual milk. I loved living the way I wanted to live. Then I'd just go on a retreat or a camp with my church and have a cool experience with Jesus, only to go back home unchanged. I grew used to that. I loved milk. See, milk is easy, it doesn't require any work. It's not solid and it's slightly satisfying. Until it's not satisfying. I came to a point in college where I realized I was settling. I was miserable.

James 1:8 talks about what it means to be double-minded. Basically it is someone who has too much of the world in them to fully enjoy the things of God and too much of God in them to fully enjoy things of the world. If you have ever heard that people who are fully engaged in a worldly lifestyle and living life without God are miserable, that's a lie. Honestly, the people who are miserable are the ones who have one foot in the world and one foot on the side of God. They never get to reap the benefit of either choice. They are stuck in the middle. For too long I was stuck in the middle; and so my experiences with God were shallow, short lived, and left me wanting. I wanted more. Oh, I had tasted the world of sin, and I saw where that would eventually lead me. I wanted to live a life seeking after God. I wanted to fully reap the benefit of a life following after Jesus. I knew it was the hard road, I knew he would take me through difficult things; but I wanted all that he had.

During those years of college I played on the basketball team. I remember one night we had a tough loss, so the coach made us practice the next morning at five a.m. Just getting up that early was miserable enough, but our coach was also determined to never let us get out-hustled again. So he blew his whistle and yelled, "On the line!" (By the way, those are words directly from the pit of hell!) So we got on the line and ran what are called "suicides."

"Again!" he yelled. Our coach just kept blowing his whistle, making us run again until most of us had thrown up. It was the most painful experience of my life. Then something amazing happened. He called us over close to him to talk. We were all huffing and puffing and he said, "Guys, look at me." We looked and he had tears in his eyes. He said, "I want you to know how much I love you and how I never want to send you out there ill-prepared again." He went on telling us his heart for us and how he longed for more for us. That morning he won us over. We knew we were loved.

○————————————————————○

Here's a passage that I really want you to read. In fact, right now run and grab a pen. I want you to circle and underline the parts of this passage that stand out to you.

Okay, got your pen? Here it is according to The Message Bible:

> By entering through faith into what God has always wanted to do for us—set us right with him, make us fit for him—we have it all together with God because of our Master Jesus. And that's not all: We throw

open our doors to God and discover at the same moment that he has already thrown open his door to us. We find ourselves standing where we always hoped we might stand—out in the wide open spaces of God's grace and glory, standing tall and shouting our praise.

There's more to come: We continue to shout our praise even when we're hemmed in with troubles, because we know how troubles can develop passionate patience in us, and how that patience in turn forges the tempered steel of virtue, keeping us alert for whatever God will do next. In alert expectancy such as this, we're never left feeling shortchanged. Quite the contrary—we can't round up enough containers to hold everything God generously pours into our lives through the Holy Spirit!

Romans 5:1-5

Here is a portion of that same passage in a different translation, the NIV. Underline or circle in this one too:

… but we also glory in our sufferings, because we know that suffering produces perseverance; perseverance, character; and character, hope. And hope does not put us to shame, because God's love has been poured out into our hearts through the Holy Spirit, who has been given to us.

Romans 5:3b-5

We were in Jamaica on a mission trip a couple of years ago. We've decided to help revitalize a village in Kingston called Water House, so we've been going there for a few years now. While we're there we always do construction, we run a VBS program, and we minister in the community. One day we sent a few students to a home of a young Jamaican woman who was sick. I say "home" but really, she lived in a shack. She had three little children, and she was so sick that she wasn't able to get out of bed for weeks. We walked in and were humbled by her circumstances. Here was this young woman with three children, no husband, no health care, and not much hope.

We surrounded her bed in awkward silence. Todd, one of our students, walked over and sat on her bed. He reached over and gently held her hand. Then, looking her in the eyes, he said, "I can see that you are very strong and God is with you." Her eyes welled up with tears, and she smiled at him while nodding her head. Then Todd loosely quoted Romans 5 to her, "God is working in you, I can see it and this hardship is going to produce in you perseverance and character, and he will fill you with a hope that will not disappoint you." Then he prayed for healing and peace and strength and for hope. By the time we left that woman looked energized, full of peace and full of hope. God was working in her and he used Todd to minister to her.

There's something that you need to know about Todd. He's had his share of hardship. Right before this trip his parents had gotten a divorce, and it really was difficult for him. Hardship either makes or breaks us, and it was making Todd. Because of hardship, God had made him full of empathy for this woman and her children. Todd was off the milk and onto the meat of what it means to be Jesus' hands and feet in this life.

When I decided in college to be totally in with God, I knew what that could mean. But I was tired of being double-minded. I was tired of being immature in my faith. I truly wanted to grow. But I've never been a person who has lacked passion. Mostly, I've been a person who has lacked follow-through. And this time I needed to change something. I needed to look closely at my life. What I noticed was that every time I went to camp or went on a retreat or mission trip, I would grow exponentially. The environment of those places set me up for spiritual awakening. It was like God was more real than he had been to me every week of the entire year combined. True spiritual passion is like that, it's an in-breaking of reality, it's a gift, it's a birthright, and it's what we were meant for. When we are in places where life slows up and the noise dissipates, all of a sudden we have the capacity to move into reality. The spiritual life awakens when we seek to discern illusion from what is real.

Now, I love speaking at camps and I have the pleasure of speaking around the country to middle school, high school, and college students. But at most camps and retreats inevitably on the last night something happens that I hate. It happens at almost every place I go. Someone gets up on stage, in front of everyone and says something to the effect of, "Hey, we've been kind of living all week together in an unreal world at this camp. But now we're getting ready to go back to reality."

> the spiritual life **awakens**
> when we seek to discern
> illusion from what is real.

I always want to jump up right after them and say, "Wrong! What they just said isn't true at all! This retreat has been the real world, where the division between each of us has dissipated, where suddenly our heads have been lifted off of ourselves and we've become aware of God and each other, where somehow things have slowed down enough to sense God and see others pursuing him. And all of a sudden we're being transparent and sharing our hearts, reading the Scriptures and worshiping God without fear of judgment. This has been the real world. This is reality. What we're getting ready to go back to is an illusion."

We live back at home in an illusion, unaware of the real.

On that long-ago day for me in college, I decided to flip the script. To change the way I'd been living. I wanted to be proactive and change the atmosphere of my life. See, atmosphere is everything. It's how you experience things in particular places and particular times. Atmosphere has helped or harmed us all in ways we probably don't even realize.

See, on a retreat I live life with people who are longing to worship God, who want to make a difference in the world, who are longing for internal and external transformation. So I needed to surround myself with others who carried that same dream, who were longing for ultimate truth and reality. I needed to live on mission and pursue God and love him with all of my heart, mind, and strength. I needed to stop playing Christian and actually become one.

And so that's what I did. I went to some of my friends and we came up with a plan. Oh, we did other things like jumping off of bridges into the river, pulling practical jokes around the campus, and constantly goofing around. But we also chose to live on mission. See I knew I couldn't follow Jesus in isolation. When my faith was a private thing, it didn't work. I knew I needed some comrades. I needed to open my daily life up to others. Taking it up a notch we found a mentor, and all of the sudden the atmosphere began to change.

Here's what happened: I started to grow. I got off the milk.

Oh, I still like milk. It's good with cookies and surprisingly delicious with popcorn. (Think I'm crazy? Try it, I swear it's great!) But I had to get off of the spiritual milk. I needed some meat. My life was craving for something solid, something with substance. My bet is you are feeling the same. You are longing for more. And here's the cool thing: God is just waiting for you to run with him.

You are ready. Truly, you are.

chapter 19

Creative Dating

I remember it like it was yesterday. I was sitting in speech class on the first day of classes and the professor was going over the syllabus, when all of a sudden it happened. Time stopped. There she was. She entered the classroom in slow motion and began to walk toward the empty chair that was next to mine. Her hair was flowing in the wind as she smiled at me and took her seat. From that moment on I knew, I just knew.

Over the next few weeks we would flirt back and forth till finally, one day, I got enough courage to ask her on a date. But I didn't want it to be just any date. This girl deserved a creative date, a date of the century, a date that she would never forget. In this chapter I have put together a few different ideas to get your brain going and to ignite some creative thinking for your next date.

So I took her on good dates. Lots of them. Once, I set up a candlelit dinner in a bathroom. I know, it sounds ridiculous and kind of gross, but it was awesome. It went so well that I would pull this date out again every once in a while as an ongoing surprise for her. See, the administration building or the auditorium are often not being used later in the evenings. So I would ask her to meet me somewhere on campus, tell her I forgot something and needed to go grab it. That was my line, and we'd head into the building with the decorated bathroom.

I'd go into the bathroom and come back out. "Oh, you've gotta see this," I'd say to her, and so she'd follow me in where there would be lights flickering (Christmas lights work great!) around the mirrors and romantic music playing (near the men's urinal, naturally) and set before her would be a beautiful candlelit dinner with all of the fixin's—usually brought in with a little help from friends. (You know, scented candles might be a good idea considering the setting.)

And by the way, that girl in speech class? The one I took on dates to abandoned bathrooms? It totally worked out. We are still together twenty-four years later.

So I put down some date ideas to get your creativity flowing.

1. Anywhere Picnic. Grab food from the cafeteria and a blanket and take it anywhere:

> park
> car
> rooftop
> office
> hallway
> empty pool
> cornfield
> under an overpass

radio tower
inside a dumpster
golf course
(You get the idea.)

2. Five-Star Fancy. Tell your date to dress well—you're going out! Have a friend act as a chauffeur and drive you both to your favorite fast food restaurant instead. Have your chauffeur (or another friend) go in first and set the table with a beautiful spread: flowers, china, real silverware, etc. The chauffeur can then bring you inside to be seated, where he or she becomes your waiter or waitress. The menu should have every selection of your location written out elegantly, ready for you to order. The waiter then takes your order to the counter and pays for it. When the food is ready, they remove it from the plastic and paper and serve it on the china—soda goes into champagne flutes, ketchup into little fancy dishes, etc. (By the way, this date can easily be taken to your local mall's food court for more options and a change of scenery!)

3. Mystery Drive. Go on a drive together, only each time you come to a red light, flip a coin: heads you go straight, tails you turn. Flip it again to find out which way to turn. Flip the coin to find out other things: where you should eat, where you should get dessert, and what movie you should see, etc.

4. Buy Some Fun. Give your date ten dollars and ask him or her to spend every penny in the mall or a dollar store, buying things that you can do together. Your date will probably buy coloring books and jacks and other fun toys. Then spend the evening using what you bought together.

5. Vroom-Vroom. Go test drive a car together. Try to find the fanciest car dealer around. (And drive safely!)

6. Creation Contest. Have a sculpting contest with Play-doh. Pick up a bunch of colors at a local toy store. Now have a sculpting contest. (When inappropriate things start to be sculpted, you'll know you're bored and it's time to stop and move on to something else.)

8. Sail Away. Head to a lake or bay and rent a small sailboat. This can run around twenty-five dollars or so for an hour, depending on your location. Pack a lunch and have a blast sailing the open water. Throw out an anchor and swim or explore an island together.

9. Just Move. For those who are in a relationship, go do something active together. Go hiking, play tennis, train for a race, run in a race, take a yoga class, go biking, join a volleyball league, go horseback riding, take a spin class, go do Zumba …

Now it's time to create. Make up your own date ideas and write them here …

the great thing, if one can,
is to stop regarding all of the unpleasant things
as interruptions of one's 'own' or 'real' life.
the truth is of course
that what one calls the interruptions
are precisely one's **real life**—
the life GOD is sending one day by day.
c. s. lewis
the collected works of c. s. lewis

chapter 20

The (Other) "D" Word

One day my friends and I were hiking out in the Tennessee Valley. Winter was coming to an end and spring was emerging right before our eyes. We walked along the riverside up the dirt trail and headed through thick green forest. We came upon a portion of the river that was kind of an inlet, where the water was slow moving and giant fish were gathering. I couldn't believe my eyes and I shouted, "What are those?"

Then all of my friends looked at me like I was crazy. They said, "Brock, have you never seen a goldfish?"

"Those aren't goldfish. I know goldfish," I protested. "Goldfish are two inches long, you buy them at the store, take them home, they die two days later, and then you flush them down the toilet.

I know goldfish and those aren't goldfish!"

Then they took pity on me and explained that goldfish only grow in size according to their environment. They have an enzyme that releases and manages their growth. If you put them in a small bowl, they stay small. But if they are free and live in a vast river like the one we had stumbled upon, then they become giants. Environment is everything to them.

We continued hiking and had an amazing day, but I couldn't get the goldfish out of my mind. Later that night I was reading Luke 9:23. It's a verse I have read hundreds of times but I never noticed one of the most important words in the entire Bible. Here's the verse:

> Then Jesus said to them all: "Whoever wants to be my disciple must deny themselves and take up their cross **DAILY** and follow me."
>
> Luke 9:23

Now again, I had read this verse and heard people talk about it for most of my life. But for whatever reason, it stood out to me in a brand new way this time. See, I had never seen the word *daily* before. In reality, I thought this verse was about giving Jesus my life. If I wanted to follow him I needed to make a choice to pick up my cross and follow him for the rest of my life. The problem is that I really don't even know what that means. How do you give someone your life? Aren't you setting yourself up to fail?

But what I can do is give him my day. I can worship him today. I can honor him with my choices today. I can choose him today. I can wake up tomorrow and give him that day. See, in the environment of daily, I can grow.

So I started looking into this a bit more and what I found encouraged me.

There are *dailies* all over the Bible:

> Give us this week our weekly bread?
> *No. Give us this day our daily bread.*
> Your mercies are new every month?
> *No. Your mercies are new every morning.*
> Pick up your cross yearly and follow me?
> *No way. "Pick up your cross daily and follow me."*

This was transformative for me. Daily was the exact environment my relationship with Jesus needed. So I stopped worrying about tomorrow. I don't know if I can please God tomorrow or next week or a year from now, but today I will. Today I choose him. Today is yours Jesus. Then at the end of that day I sit back on my bed and I think, "Okay, Lord, how'd I do?" Then I just quickly ask him to forgive me of those times during that day where I slipped up. See, I keep short accounts with relationships that I care about. I talk to my wife daily. I spend time with her, and when I mess up, I quickly make things right. The same should be true with any relationships we care about.

At that time I had heard a friend talk about how he was living out this daily thing. He said that every morning he'd put his two feet on the ground and give Jesus his day, but then he'd also give him one area of his life that he was struggling with. Maybe he was struggling with anger. So he would give him his thoughts or his emotions that day. This is what he'd pray: "Jesus, today is yours, and I give you my anger. Rein in my emotions today." When he told me this, I thought it was huge! See, maybe you're struggling with what you are looking at or with your worries or with your words—you just give him one thing, one day at a time. Initially, it might seem silly, but if you stay committed to the environment of daily, you will see character build and you will live more and more aware of God's spirit.

I started doing this daily thing, but my friend had wisely cautioned against trying to make it alone. He'd said that everyone needs at least two people in their lives: Everyone needs a peer and everyone needs a mentor.

It's like when you go body surfing. When you first go to the beach everyone runs onto the sand and places their towels, coolers, and umbrellas on their spot. Then, if you're like me, you and a buddy head out to the water. And you're out there together playing and riding the waves, looking out for each other and cheering each other on. It's a blast! Until you look up at the beach and think everyone has left. All of the blankets are gone and the umbrella is missing. You think, "What the heck? Did everyone seriously just leave without telling us?" But then you realize that, no, it's you who have moved. You've drifted way down shore. And so you and your friend have to get out of the water and hike it way back up to where your stuff is. And that's why you need someone a little older, a little wiser, who can help keep you from drifting. You have your friend out there in the water doing life together, but then you've got someone on the beach helping the two of you not drift too far away. Your mentor acts as a lifeguard, yelling: "You've gone too far! Come back where I can see you! You've drifted out of the boundaries!" They remind us that we have to stay humble, that our spiritual lives need wisdom and nurturing. That was huge for me.

See, every day we get up and we give Jesus our day. We live life with people who are longing for the same things, and we seek consistent wisdom from a sage—an older person who has much to give us. We can grow in that environment. We can become everything we long to become. One day at a time.

do not be afraid, for i have redeemed you;
ihave called you by your name, you are mine.
you are precious in my eyes,
because you are honored and **i love you**...
the mountains may depart, the hills be shaken,
but my love for you will never leave,
and my covenant of peace will never be shaken.
isaiah 43:1, 4; 54:10

chapter 21

Stories of God's Pursuit

Last night we all sat in my living room, ate pizza, laughed, and slowly started to open up. It happens like this every week. We eat, talk junk to each other, and then something happens. Seriously, it happens almost every time we're together. They come in stressed, distracted, and spiritually empty but by the end of the evening they are praying for each other, getting filled up, and they head back into the storm called life. But they arrive the following week dry to the bone all over again. These guys are all getting ready to graduate high school now and each of them carries hopes and fears and joys along with so many sorrows. The journey is ending and just beginning all at the same time.

On this night, I head up to bed, but I just can't sleep. Their struggles stay with me, and I can't seem to shake them. See, I'm a youth worker and I absolutely love it. I'm honored to care for middle school, high school, and college students. I couldn't imagine doing anything else. But I have to tell you something, I think about quitting almost every week. See, I'm one of those people who can't leave my work at the office. Well, to be honest, I'm rarely at the office, but you get the idea. I carry with me the stories of these young people. Many of the preteens, teenagers, and young adults in my life live in messy home environments or they carry hurts, addictions, and they just really struggle with so much. And I completely get it. It isn't easy growing up in today's world let alone following Jesus in it, even for me. But there are moments I just want to move to the Caribbean and call it quits.

The problem for me is that then true living would cease. Journeying with these amazing people would end. I'd turn inward on myself, and I'd stopped being apart of what God is doing. Life would become about me, and so I'd never see what I consistently see. I'd never see God breakthrough all of the mess, the junk and hold and heal and fill and inspire and bring change to these amazing lives.

This morning I had breakfast with an eleventh grade guy. About a year ago he felt like God was calling him to work in the justice field, bringing hope to the hopeless and setting captives and slaves free. He felt that somehow, through this, he would be a light in very dark places. Initially I thought, "Well, that's an amazing and God-sized kind of dream!" I guess all I was just really hoping was that he wouldn't forget once he got out of high school, and that he'd actually go and do it.

I think God may have been thinking the same thing, because shortly after this revelation he was at church. He was praying that God would give him a picture of what he wanted him to do.

Later that night at church a woman walked up to him and said that God had given her a picture of a little girl in a dark and dirty room when all of a sudden this guy—this eleventh grade young man—busted through the door and carried the little girl to safety. This woman felt like her vision showed that God was going to use this amazing young guy someday to be salt and light to the world. He would be a voice of hope to many. And immediately he came running over to me, overwhelmed with joy at God answering his prayer and showing him his calling.

Now if you're like me, you kind of doubt this vision—if that's what we want to call it—was actually from God. I mean, surely it's got to be coincidental! Sebastian Moore, author of *The Contagion of Jesus*, once wrote, "In religion, there always lurks the fear that we invented the story of God's love" (Orbis Books, 2008).

God always leaves us that choice. But what I would say, from my own experiences, is that Jesus just keeps revealing himself to me and to the youth I minister to who are in way over their heads in a difficult world. It just seems like, when we pause and when we are still and quiet, when we take the time to open our lives up, God speaks to the deepest strata of our souls.

When I have those thoughts of quitting and doing something more normal and less tormenting, I'm reminded of stories of God running after us. I love that he runs after us. I'm addicted to being a part of what he's doing, and so I can't walk away. I can't quit.

In fact, you're reading this right now and there are almost certainly very difficult things happening around you. I bet there are moments when you have wondered if you should just throw in the spiritual towel. Like, maybe the God stuff is great for other people, but you wonder if it may not be for you. My prayer is that you would hold on; that you would continue to open your life up to the God who is at work. Even now inside of your heart and mind he is waking you up to something.

Recently we had a teenage girl share with our congregation. She talked about her struggle to follow Jesus at home. But on mission trips and at camps she experiences him all the time. She said that life back home is too busy and too noisy to hear God, but somehow when she takes the time to get away she finds him. I looked at her and said, "Wow, Jen, what you just said reminds me of that verse where Jesus says, 'When you seek me, you will find me.'" She looked at me, there on the stage, with the microphone, in front of the whole church and said, "Wow, I've never thought of it that way. I never knew that Jesus was always there, and the moment I pick my head up and look for him, I find him!" God is pursuing our hearts.

> even now inside of your heart and mind
> he is **waking** you up to something.

My little gang of brothers who come to my house every Tuesday night are discovering this. It's like they come in from the cold and the rain and they get warm in my house. And by the end, their hearts and minds have thawed out enough to see God and experience his presence. He so wants them to walk out the door with him though. But nonetheless, God is relentless in his pursuit of them.

He's even pursuing those who aren't seeking him. He has a heart for the ones who couldn't give a rip about spirituality. Yesterday I was in a meeting with a few people, some adults and some students. We were planning how we might serve local schools and be a blessing to our community. We started talking about how each of us came to faith. One of the teenage guys in this meeting, who about a year ago was rebellious and completely against Christianity, shared. He said that whenever religion came up, he would just rip it apart and belittle anyone who believed in God. But now he was sitting in a meeting talking about how we can serve the schools in our city and be God's blessing to them. Amazing! It reminded me of the story of St. Paul. Here's a man dead set against the early church, with a passion to get rid of this new faith. But God had other plans. He takes a young arrogant zealot and turns him into a humble servant of Jesus Christ.

In the same way we sat in this meeting talking about how God *kapow!*'d this young guy. It wasn't me, it wasn't any leaders, it was God. In fact, the first time he came to our youth group I got off the stage and thought, "That was the worst talk I may have ever given." I felt like a failure. But this kid came up to me and asked to meet with me over coffee. We met a week later and he told me that for some reason, when I was speaking, he felt something and it kind of freaked him out. I gave him a book to read, and he devoured it in about two days. He called me up and said, "Okay, I'm in." This kid has not been the same since. God wanted him. God has a heart for this young man. God is on the move, and he has a vision for people everywhere, and he has a heart for you too.

I have to tell you something, despite the rocky road of trying to keep up with Jesus, I am just so grateful and overwhelmed by his goodness. I'm blown away by how he consistently shows up, despite me and my narcissism.

Many of us look at this broken world and it just feels like the spiritual temperature is that of an Alaskan winter. But under the surface God is working. God is working in your friends' lives too. You may not see it, but he is. And he is pursuing you with the kind of transformative love that if you ever fully encounter it, you just might never be the same again.

But in order to see that transformative love, in order to experience it, we must remember that it's all about proximity. If I am close to Jesus, I see more. It's also about my proximity to others. My life is my relationship with God, and everything that God does in me spills over to those I'm around. If I'm not spilling, then I'm not truly living.

But about a year ago I had worked myself into the ground. There was a long season of working with no days off and the constant demand of writing and speaking, plus the ministry at my church was overwhelming. I got to the point where I felt so dry in my soul, I felt like I was about to crack. I knew what I needed. I needed some R&R and some alone time with Jesus. So I got into my Jeep and headed for the mountains. Deep into the northern part of Connecticut is a secret swimming hole. No one knows about it—except for, like, everyone. But it was in the middle of the day and I parked in the foothills and headed out for a long hike. It was at the end of the winter and the snow had just melted. The river was high and fast and loud, and I hiked alongside of the roaring water for a couple of miles. I stopped at the foot of one of the most beautiful waterfalls you've ever seen. And the mist of the falls was in the air, surrounding me. I stood there and my soul was soaking it all in. In that moment I sensed Jesus say, "Brock, I've got you."

Those words just kept reverberating in my mind and heart. "Brock, I've got you. I've got your young people, your ministry, everything! I've got you." I just stood there and made a choice to trust him with everything. Knowing that while I slept, he wouldn't. When I can't always be there for the youth I serve, he will be. When I don't quite measure up, he does. He's got me.

So I headed back to the car and drove home. The next morning we were in prayer as a church staff when Dave, our worship leader, looked at me and said, "Brock, I feel like I have a word from the Lord for you."

Now, normally when people say that, I'm kind of cynical. This time I was open; it was Dave and he's awesome. "What's the word Dave? I'm ready," I said.

Dave shot back with this: "Brock, God is telling you, 'I've got you, you don't need to worry, I've got everything!' " I couldn't believe it.

And as we close this chapter, I just feel like you need to know that God is with you too. His favor is upon you, and you can trust him. You can rest in the fact that he's got you.

He's got you. You don't need to worry. God's heart is for you.

we should be astonished at the goodness of GOD,
stunned that he should bother to call us by name,
our mouths wide open at **his love**,
bewildered that at this very moment
we are standing on holy ground.
brennan manning
the ragamuffin gospel

chapter 22

Surprised by a Song

I gathered my things and stuffed them in my backpack. We were leaving for a weekend hiking trip, a trip that promised an underground river, bonfires, and just hanging out with friends. I couldn't wait.

We'd heard legends about a river up in the mountain that ran along the cliffs and then disappeared for twenty-five yards underground, only to come springing up on the other side of the summit crossing. I couldn't wait to find it and try riding it like I had heard in the stories told in the dorm rooms of a small Tennessee college. So we grabbed our stuff and headed out for a few hours' drive that led us to a parking lot at the base of the mountain.

It was a warm day with a cool breeze, the kind of day where you're not sure whether to pack your jacket or wear it. It was cold in the shade and warm where the pockets of sunlight found their way between the trees. The mountains still had snow sprinkled along their edges, and there was a sweet pine smell that filled the air.

We hiked for about three hours, being led by a friend who had gotten directions from an upperclassmen. He swore that the underground river did exist and that many years ago students had actually ridden it. Finally, after heading through steep terrain and down through the valley's ridge we came to the river, took a right heading north, and trekked up the path that ran beside this fast-moving white water. And there it was. The underground river actually existed, except it seemed much bigger, faster, and scarier than I'd pictured in my head. There were huge boulder rocks throughout the river, and the water just looked cold—too cold. We stood there with the sunlight on our shoulders for probably a good five minutes before someone said, "Okay, who's first?"

I have the reputation of being pretty daring, not thinking things through very well, and basically jumping first and fearing later. So everyone volunteered me to go first. I said that I would go, but you have to understand something here, it took me fifteen minutes just to get up the nerve to jump in. And so with a yell, I jumped into the freezing cold river water and headed downstream toward the cave mouth that led, hopefully, to the other side without any major obstacles.

As I approached the underground portion of this ride, I could tell that I was going to be consumed by the water. I would need to hold my breath for the whole twenty-five yards. And then there I was, falling about ten feet into this great chasm. I took in a huge breath, closed my eyes, and hoped for the best. As I rode the rapids through this pitch-black underwater canal I could feel sticks, leaves, and muck hitting me in the face and body.

Do you remember being a little kid and playing in the pool? Remember when your friend would jump on top of you and hold you under the water till you thought you were going to die if you didn't get air immediately? That feeling is what began to consume me: complete and utter panic. I'd held my breath for only God knows how long and felt like I couldn't hold it much longer. I needed to get out of there … now. Five seconds later—which felt like about five minutes—I popped up on the other side. The jubilant screams of my friends' celebration echoed around me; and I heard the *splash, splash, splash* as they each jumped in for the ride of their lives. By the time I'd made it out of the water and onto a large rock overhanging the river, some locals had heard that dumb college boys were riding the underground river. They started to gather and watch with me on the river's edge. It was so funny to see my friends screaming and riding this thing over and over again. For me, one ride was enough, so I kneeled down and started a conversation with a little boy.

He asked me, "Why are you guys doing this?" And, honestly, I didn't have an answer for him. I hadn't thought through it very well, but I sat down with him and started telling him about the sense of adventure that we all had. He asked if we were afraid of getting hurt or even of dying. This kid just kept asking me questions that were surprisingly deep and thoughtful. Basically he was asking me my view of life in this world and what I was doing in a place like this talking to a little boy like him. It's funny how God shows up in the strangest places and in the unlikeliest people.

So there on the rock, talking with that little boy, I sensed God. In the midst of the tall pines, surrounded by the magnificent mountains, and the sound of the river flowing with my friends' laughter in the background, I sensed God. I sensed him in that place.

I wasn't looking for him but he was there, he was with us. Have you ever been in a place doing something, maybe with friends, and you just knew it was a sacred moment? It's like you get a glimpse of how life is supposed to be lived.

Maybe during those moments you get a glimpse of who you really are. This is why camps and retreats are so vital. Because we live at camp the way we always wished we could live here and now. It's like our humanity is given back to us and we become our true selves. There in the quiet, under the stars, on the water, in the cabin, and at the bonfire we are finally us. But most of the time I look at myself and I am not who I want to be.

And I think back to the beginning when everything was as it should be.

Adam and Eve were who they were created to be and had the potential to become even greater. There was no insecurity, addiction, lust, hatred, or even regret. God was as close to them as possible—walking, talking, laughing, and telling wild stories about how he made the hippopotamus, and the kangaroo, the orca whale, and the eagle. They would head out together on adventures for days at a time with no relational tension and no fear between them, full of wonder at God's creation.

It blows me away to think of life in that place. It makes me long for the time when Christ returns and renews all of his creation. It makes me long for the time when Jesus fixes, once and for all, what we have destroyed. And that takes us to the tragic part of the story. When Adam and Eve rebelled, and sin, brokenness, separation, and division took over. Now sin rules and it comes so natural for me. It's natural for me *not* to love others more than I love myself, and it's natural to place my needs ahead of everyone else's—to contribute to the ruin and the dysfunction. But herein lies what is so surprising: The writers of the holy scriptures called the message of the Bible Good News. Well, I've been looking into this, and I think that maybe the Good News is actually better news than we ever dreamed.

When many of us think of the Bible, we think about how God will one day judge us with harshness and with anger. We imagine he looks at us and says, "I'm so disappointed in you, and I want nothing to do with you!" Like an angry father who wants nothing to do with his child; because the child isn't performing or behaving in a matter than will make him, as a dad, look good. But take a look at this passage:

> During the reign of King Josiah, the LORD said to me, "Have you seen what faithless Israel has done? She has gone up on every high hill and under every spreading tree and has committed adultery there. I thought that after she had done all this she would return to me but she did not, and her unfaithful sister Judah saw it.
>
> Jeremiah 3:6-7

The language in this passage is very romantic. It describes God as a husband who is head over heels in love with his bride, Israel. But his bride has not only committed adultery she's done it publicly, in front of the whole world. So this is where we would expect divorce and judgment. We'd definitely think that the marriage would be over.

But check out how the story ends:

> The LORD appeared to us in the past, saying: "I have loved you with an everlasting love; I have drawn you with loving-kindness. I will build you up again and you will be rebuilt, O Virgin Israel. Again you will take up your tambourines and go out to dance with the

joyful. Again you will plant vineyards on the hills of Samaria; the farmers will plant them and enjoy their fruit.

Jeremiah 31:3-5

God calls his adulterous bride a virgin! Has he lost his mind? She has sinned publicly, humiliating him, not caring at all about their commitment and love for each other. Yet God moves beyond her unfaithfulness and pursues her with his love.

And you know what, he says something similar to you and to me, "I don't see you by your failures, addictions, and screw-ups. I have a plan to restore you and make you into who you were created to be. My love for you goes beyond your performance or your behavior. I am for you and I will not give up on you."

> it's like our humanity is given back to us and we become our **true** selves.

When I think of God in this light I'm blown away. I think about my past, my mistakes, and how—because of those things—people have written me off and labeled me as worthless. I think of the abuse I have experienced and at times how I have blamed God for how others have mistreated me. Boy, have I been wrong. When I study the scriptures and experience God firsthand, I discover a God who is broken and sad over the condition of his creation. I discover how he longs for his creation to stop the madness of abuse and hatred.

My mom, Carol, is an amazing woman, who was raised in a difficult home environment. From the time she was a little girl her parents would verbally, physically, and emotionally abuse her. She felt like she never measured up, like she just wasn't good enough.

As a child she had an unusual gifting for music. She was able to play anything she heard on the piano and would frequently make up her own lyrics. She was regularly asked to accompany singers in church, but her parents made it clear that they disliked her singing by making fun of her whenever she sang. Imagine being named Carol, which means "song," and being mocked whenever you lived out the very calling of your name. It's ironic that my mom has since sung in commercials, on television, and was the lead singer of a band that had a top-ten hit on pop radio. Yet her parents treated her as an embarrassment to the family. Abuse is an amazing thing. It skews the way we see others and the way we see ourselves.

The story hits an all-time low when, not long ago, her parents invited her to their home. It had been years since they'd even spoken to her, so she went to visit them with high hopes for reconciliation. However, from the moment she got there the realization of their true intentions hit her in the face. They began to walk her around the house showing her all the things that she wouldn't inherit when they died. They told her they didn't truly see her as their daughter and that she'd get nothing. Then they said, "And we don't want you singing at our funeral either."

Have you ever seen someone cry so hard that when you look at them, with tears streaming down their face, you actually feel a piece of the pain they're experiencing? It was an overwhelming feeling to see my mother come home from that trip broken, hurt, and desperate to hear she was worthy of love.

Here was my amazing mother—a professional musician and, more importantly, a kind and caring woman—who couldn't seem to get the love of her parents. But God knows her pain and the insecurities that she carries and, as a good father, he showed up. Not only did he show up, He fully redeemed my mom's story. She returned home to our house and was asked to play the piano and sing at the end of that Sunday morning church service. As she was playing, a teenager came up to her and quietly sat next to her on the piano bench. It seemed strange, but what happened next is stranger still. This young man whispered these words to my mother: "Carol, I don't know why I'm supposed to tell you this, but God wanted you to know that he loves it when you sing."

How great is the love of God? How amazing and detailed and aware is his love for us? To what lengths will he go to prove you are treasured, honored, and that your future is amazing? He will go down any path, climb over any obstacle, endure any pain—even death on the cross—to express his love to you.

Hear the word of the Lord:

> Do not be afraid, for I have redeemed you; I have called you by your name, you are mine. You are precious in my eyes, because you are honored and I love you… The mountains may depart, the hills be shaken, but my love for you will never leave, and my covenant of peace will never be shaken.
>
> Isaiah 43:1, 4; 54:10

This is how God sees you. You were meant to live for so much more than you could ever imagine. But how will you respond? Today, please know this: The glimpses that you get of your potential, of your greatness, are actually the true picture of who you really are. Those glimpses are the picture of who you were designed to be. When you love, serve, and place others ahead of yourself you are seeing God in you. He is making you, from the inside out, to look like his son Jesus. And guess what? You do.

Questions to Ponder

What's the biggest adventure that you've ever been on? What did it show you about yourself?

Have you ever been surprised by God's thoughtfulness or grace?

Have you ever sensed that God was with you in the middle of a painful experience?

Looking at the Isaiah passages above, we see how Israel, in essence, had an affair—they publicly rejected God in front of the world. And yet God lovingly took them back and accepted them and forgave them. Why do you think God would show such love and mercy?

How do you think God sees or defines you?

Reread 1 Corinthians 6:19. *Rewrite it in your own words.*

How should the reality of this passage change the way you live?

GOD is willing
to **walk the earth**,
again incarnate in us.
eugenia price
early will i seek thee

chapter 23

The Overlap

As I've shared, as a youth pastor I have had my share of sleepless nights. And not just because of middle school lock-ins, but because of living life with students and walking with them through the pain of neglect, abuse, mistakes, and consequence, I have had the weight of hearing their stories press down upon me. Many of the details they have shared with me have tortured me late at night, when I am alone with my thoughts. Let me share with you one such story.

When she first walked into the room it appeared like everything was just fine. This 13-year-old girl had such energy and excitement about her, but through the façade of laughter and smiles was pain beyond anything you could ever imagine. Something terribly wrong was brewing under the surface.

I had heard from her grandfather that she would be joining our middle school group and that what had brought her to us was rejection in a form that I, personally, struggled to grasp. So immediately we went to work getting her connected, giving her a mentor, and just making sure that we created an environment where she could experience the warmth of God. After about nine months had passed, she came up to me in the church bus and bluntly asked, "Brock, why didn't she pick me?"

About a year prior to her arrival to us, her mother had taken a live-in boyfriend. It started well, but inevitably things went downhill. He began to pick up the bottle each night, and with each drink he would become more and more angry. When I think of how it was described to me, it reminds me of a volatile pit-bull that seems nice at first, but you know that something, anything, might just set him off. As the weeks turned into months the dysfunction grew, and he began to beat her mother. Seeing your mom get beaten on a regular basis by a raging lunatic twice your size must be horrific; and the sense of anger, panic, and powerlessness must be unimaginable. But this little girl was not having it and began to stick up for her mom. How did this man react to a little girl defending her mother? He began to beat her as well. Eventually some neighbors and friends reported this to social services. This series of events brought her mother before the judge, who did not mince words, "This case is simple, lady. You need to pick either your daughter or your boyfriend." And so the choice was made.

"Brock, why didn't my mom pick me?"

Have you ever been asked a question that you have no clue how to answer? I was at a loss for words. Under my breath I prayed a simple prayer, "God give me something here, PLEASE."

I paused and then asked her a question instead. "Did you ever ask God, maybe when you were in bed at night and the lights were out and all was quiet, 'God, if you're real, you've got to help me. You have got to get me out of this situation.' Did you ever pray a prayer like that?"

"Of course I did, many times," she said.

I took in a deep breath, "Well, do you think he answered?"

She responded hesitantly and with thoughtfulness, "No, I don't think so. But what do you think, Brock?"

I said, "Well, I think he did answer you. When you were praying in your room at night and asking him to get you out of that horrible situation, he not only heard you, he answered you. He moved and plucked you out of that place, and he brought you here to us. He heard you those nights in the dark when you were crying out to him."

At this point we were both crying, and then she said with a whisper, "I never knew. I never realized that God cared."

In Genesis, sin entered the world and changed everything. We are still feeling its effects. We rebelled from God in the garden, and we are still experiencing the fallout from that choice to this day. We are still feeling the broken relationship with God firsthand. We see it in our homes, in our parents' marriages, at school, and at work. We see it all over the place and all over the world. Here is the overwhelming truth: **We are lost without God.**

Fortunately God was not satisfied with this new cursed arrangement either. He was broken over it and he longed to repair and restore everything—bringing it back to the full potential of the garden, bringing us back to himself.

I was thinking about how Adam and Eve must have felt about it all. Can you imagine what they were experiencing when this sin and rebellion was passed to their children? Can you comprehend even an ounce of their regret when they saw their oldest son morph into a murderer? Can you imagine the pain of knowing how it once was in the garden and that all of humanity would never experience that kind of closeness and intimacy with the Creator?

But can you imagine how God must have felt?

Having a daughter has truly changed my life. It has given me a small glimpse into the love of God for us. My favorite time of the day was when I got to put my little girl to bed at night. I'd go in and tell her stories about bears and monkeys, when she was little, and how amazing shc is. I remember when she started third grade and we took her to school for her first day. I just love the first day of school. All the kids have their new outfits on and there is an excitement and nervous energy in the air. The room smells like Elmer's glue and the desks are neatly arranged with children's names on them. There's something special and memorable about seeing your teacher for the first time and reuniting with old friends that you haven't seen since the previous school year.

So we were shocked when we picked up our daughter to find that she'd had a lousy first day. She began to tell us that she didn't know anyone in her class and all the other girls knew each other from the previous school year. You always want a friend or two to make it to your next year's class, but that unfortunately hadn't happened. So she ate lunch alone, played by herself at recess, and to top it all off a boy called her stupid. I asked what the boy's name was and his address, so that I could drive over and handle it man to man. (She wouldn't give his information, but I think I could've taken him.)

I could feel the heaviness in her heart. She didn't want to go to school the next day or, for that matter, ever. So I started to pray that God would give me a moment to speak life and vision to my precious little girl.

I don't know, maybe it's the quiet and the peacefulness you feel at that time of the evening, but I just love it. The lights are dim, the neighborhood is quiet, and there is an unusual peace in the house, a stillness. The time came that evening for me to tuck my daughter in. I went to her room hoping to help my little girl not feel so burdened about tomorrow.

From the moment she was born, my wife and I decided that we would tell our daughter who she really is. I mean, culture is going to tell her who she is. Her friends will have an opinion, and I bet her successes and her failures might define her. But most of those things are lies and tend to cause us not to live up to our true potential. How we see ourselves is so important. We have made sure our daughter looks to us for affirmation and identity.

I walked into her bedroom that night, all the while praying under my breath, "God, help me to give her vision for who she is, for her school, for making new friends, and even for the little jerk who called her stupid."

We had begun our evening ritual of singing, scratching her back, and praying together when suddenly my daughter looked at me and said, "Daddy, tell me who I am again." I couldn't believe my ears! God had answered my prayer right on the spot. I had the privilege, there in her room, sitting on her bed, to tell my daughter the truth. I got to tell her how God sees her and how he has made her to do amazing things with her life.

My eyes well up with tears as I think of that story. I know she will grow up, make mistakes, and possibly even fall away from

God. She might even reject my love, but I have to tell you something: No matter what, my love for her will never change. It will not waver, it will be steady, and for all time. My little girl and this love I carry with me for her has given me a tiny glimpse into how God must feel about us.

Adam and Eve were living a life without the intimacy with God that they once experienced in the garden. This was not—it is not—how it was supposed to be. There is this huge chasm between the Creator and the created that God is achingly desperate to bridge. God didn't want us to be distant from him. God doesn't want you and I to live a life away from him. And so God, from the beginning, devised a plan to bring us back to him.

One of the first things God did to cross the divide was to set up a temple system. He put into motion a plan where he and mankind could meet again. Theologians call the temple of God the overlap (N. T. Wright, *Simply Christian*). There were unofficial places like this before the temple was built where God reached out to commune with us, but the temple became the permanent place where heaven and earth literally met. This was where God's presence dwelt and where mankind could get a glimpse of what the garden must have been like.

But, honestly, this wasn't good enough. It wasn't good enough for the people at that time, and it wasn't good enough for God. For God it was a first step, a temporary solution to a horrible problem. There was a pivotal second step to restore all of creation, to renew and fix what was broken, to bring heaven back to earth. In order to redeem all of creation God sent his son, Jesus, to become the overlap and then to do something unheard of.

In Jesus, people found hope and healing. They found intimacy with God, just like it was in the Garden and then in the temple—men, women, and children walking and talking with God again.

That's how it's supposed to be. But sometimes things get worse before they get better.

God in the flesh went to the cross and died.

That's the part of the story even the disciples didn't understand. But in this amazing story, Jesus died our death. He paid the price for our rebellion. Romans 5:10 tell us that we were enemies with God and—so he wouldn't have to imprison, punish, and destroy us as his enemies—his Son took our place, dying our death, serving our sentence. Jesus as the overlap was killed and vanished for three days only to rise again, fully alive, resurrected.

After Jesus' resurrection, he hung out with his disciples for about a month. Over a thousand people touched him, were ministered to by him, and were given the vision to spread the Good News of how we could be a part of bringing heaven to earth. Then Jesus ascended into paradise, but the disciples didn't want him to leave. (Of course they didn't want him to leave!) Jesus was the overlap and when he left, so did the presence of God.

But Jesus had to go, and they were left empty, like they felt before they'd met him. But what they didn't understand was that if he stayed then the miracle of all miracles couldn't happen. Jesus said it this way, "If I stay then the Father can't send his Spirit to indwell each of you" (John 16:7; author's paraphrase). This is where the Good News becomes better news than we ever imagined.

> Do you not know that your body is a temple of the Holy Spirit, who is in you, whom you have received from God? You are not your own ...
>
> 1 Corinthians 6:19

What the disciples didn't realize was that the Holy Spirit would come and make them the temple, the dwelling place of God. They would essentially become the overlap, the place where heaven and earth would meet. They would become a place where people would find hope, life, and light. But this is still not the end of the story.

Listen well to this: You continue the overlap; you are the overlap in this age. You are the temple of God. You are where heaven and earth come together. When God looks at you he is so proud. His hand is upon you, his spirit is inside of you, and your future is amazing ...

———————————————————————

"Daddy, tell me who I am again."

You are the dwelling place of God.

Questions to Ponder

How do you feel about being the dwelling place of God, the temple?

How should this change the way you see yourself, the way you live, and the way you see your future?

Read 1 Corinthians 6:19-20. *How do you feel about this statement: "You are not your own; you were bought at a price."*

Does God have the right to be the leader of your life?

Considering how he sees you and how he loves you, can you trust him to lead you?

legalism says GOD will love us if we change.
the gospel says GOD will change us
because he **loves** us.
tullian tchividjian

chapter 24

Beautifully Awake

I'd seen movies and television programs of children being born, so when my wife was rushed into the delivering room I was expecting a gruesome, loud, and frantic scene. You know the kind … the baby comes out, it has weird gunk all over it, it's screaming, and it looks, well, ugly. And you're thinking, "Hose that thing off, clean it up, 'cause I'm not touching it!" So this was what I expected. But it wasn't like that at all.

When our daughter was born the room was peaceful and quiet. She was laying there in the doctor's hands so quiet and beautiful, not moving, not moving at all. My first thought was that she was not alive, maybe a stillborn baby. It is strange how fear is one of the first emotions someone feels when they are not in control. But the doctor looked at me, holding our little girl in his hands, and whispered, "Mr. Morgan, shhh ... your daughter is asleep."

She wasn't screaming, gross, or ugly. No, she was the most beautiful thing I had ever seen. From the moment I first saw her I loved her. It is an indescribable kind of love. It is a love I never even knew existed. I now understand how much my parents must love me.

What I felt as my daughter was lying there sleeping in the doctor's hands was so unexpected. The nurse asked me to cut the cord and handed me the scissors. (I tried to talk them into allowing me to bite the cord in two. Any manly man would do it this way, I thought, but they were not having it.) Reluctantly I cut the cord with what looked like weed trimmers, and as soon as I did, she woke up. Her eyes opened, color came to her skin, she began to stretch, and she looked around the room.

They say babies can't see anything when they're first born, but I swear, it was like she became aware of her environment and our eyes actually met. Father and daughter looked at each other for the first time. She woke up from her sleep and became aware of something other than herself—she became beautifully awake. And I remember looking at this little girl, my little girl, and feeling that I had just experienced the divine. Seeing her wake up from her sleep was one of the most transforming experiences of my life.

> For it is light that makes everything visible.
> This is why it is said: "Wake up, O sleeper, rise from the dead, and Christ will shine on you."
> Ephesians 5:14

Some biblical scholars say that Ephesians 5:14 is actually an ancient hymn of the early church that was sung when a new believer was baptized. See, baptism signified enlightenment. It was symbolic of a person coming into the light, waking up from their sleep of carelessness and sin, and living not just in the light but also as light itself. Jesus actually calls us the light of the world; a city on a hill; salt and flavor to a world broken, lost, and asleep. In Psalm 3, there is a prayer where the psalmist calls God the lifter of his head. In other words, "God, you make me aware of yourself, others, and this mission to be light. You lift my head. My eyes have mostly just been on me: my needs, my issues, my feelings, my longings, my stuff, and my desires. You have made me aware of yourself and now I am forever changed. I see in a whole new way, and I am no longer the main subject of my life, my story. You are."

When I was a kid I thought that life was all about me. You know: my friends, my activities, the girl I liked, and the stuff that I wanted. I once heard a famous speaker say that when he was a kid he thought life was a movie starring him. How did he know this? Because he was in every scene. As you get older you hopefully begin to wake up to a larger reality, a bigger purpose.

In life, God is longing to wake us up to himself and to others. He wants us in on the action. He wants us wide-eyed and fully awake! It is like Isaiah when he actually meets God and falls on his face before him. He says in Isaiah 6:5: " 'Woe to me!' I cried. 'I am ruined! For I am a man of unclean lips, and I live among a people of unclean lips, and my eyes have seen the King, the LORD Almighty.' "

It seems to be the first time Isaiah had noticed his brokenness and the brokenness of his friends, his family, and the world. His head was lifted. He became aware of something other than himself. He became aware of God and the world's need for renewal.

Later in the Isaiah story, God purifies and forgives Isaiah and then allows Isaiah to overhear a conversation. In verse 8 it says,

"Then I heard the voice of the Lord saying, 'Whom shall I send? And who will go for us?' And I said, 'Here am I. Send me!' "
Did you get that? God is looking for someone to go; someone to represent him; and someone to bring hope, healing, and light to the world. And Isaiah, after having this amazing experience with God, looks at him and says, "I'm glad you forgave me, but now I've got some sinning to do."

No. Not at all.

The response to having God lift your head is that you go. You must go. You think, "I've got to be a part of what he's doing. I can't just sit here." Once you wake up, you have to get up. And so Isaiah gets up and becomes part of God's transforming work in the world. He lives a life aware and awakened to others and to the heartbeat of God. He no longer sleeps life away, no longer just sits there. No, he's awake, he's alive, maybe for the very first time in his life. He now has a reason, a mission, and a purpose. And so do you.

It wasn't long ago that I sat around a fire pit with some of the senior guys in my youth group when one of them looked at me and said, "Brock, we want you to know we're with you. We are ready! We're in for the adventure and we want to join this journey with you!" I was blown away. See, they are waking up to who they really are, and I'm so glad that God is revealing himself to them—that he is lifting their heads.

They want to live a life awake to him and to others. They are longing to spend every moment living with their eyes wide open. Not living so consumed by their appetites, their desires, and ... themselves.

See, when you let God lead you, you never know what's going to happen next. Adventure is waiting, and true life is right around the corner. Now don't get me wrong, it's not all peaches and cream. Life never is. There's been hard stuff, difficult stuff, sleepless nights, and times when I've been heartbroken. There have been seasons when God has felt very far away, distant, or even gone. During those times I've learned that if I just hang on, if I just stay in there, eventually breakthrough comes.

adventure is **waiting**,

and true life is right around the corner.

I have experienced God in surprising ways. He shows up, always in the nick of time, which I don't always like. Sometimes it doesn't feel quite soon enough. But my eyes have been opened to him. I've noticed and seen him in places that I never would have seen otherwise. I'm so glad that I've been awakened from my sleep. And maybe that's your prayer as well, that you would become awakened too and live this life to the fullest. Maybe you're praying—even now as you're reading—that God would do an amazing work and make you beautifully awake. Maybe you feel desperate to have your head lifted and your eyes opened and your passion ignited.

So that's my prayer for you.

May you come to know how deep and wide and huge and vast is the love of your Heavenly Father for you. May your head be lifted, may you become aware, and wake up to this amazing life that God is longing to bless you with. May your eyes be opened to God and others and may you be used in ways you never dreamed. And may you have the courage to actually do it, to pursue this God anywhere, anyhow, and at any time. My prayer is that you are surprised, even shocked, by a God who cares for you in ways you thought no one could and that he takes you to places and into relationships you never even knew existed.

When my daughter was about four years old, I held her cute chubby face in my hands and looked her in the eyes and said, "God is going to do incredible things with your life." This caught her attention, so she looked at me and said, "Daddy, what is he going to do?" I said, "Oh, sweetie, I'm not totally sure, but it's going to be good. Together we'll discover what it will be. But I can tell you this: He is going to do amazing things with you!"

And right now I want you to hear it too: God is truly going to do amazing things with your life. And you were made for this, living wide awake. It's quite a journey, but you are ready.

Transformation is waiting.

Questions to Ponder

Have you ever felt numb inside and spiritually asleep?

What can you do in the coming week to seek God and to live life awakened to him?

Who are people in your life that you can seek to help guide and encourage you?

What are you longing to see happen in your life?

Write a prayer to God expressing how you feel. Tell him everything that's on your mind after thinking through the journey ahead.

Dear Lord,

Journey Further

BOOKS

The Language of God: A Scientist Presents Evidence for Belief
by Francis Collins (Free Press, 2007)

Living with Questions
by Dale Fincher (Zondervan/Invert/YS, 2007)

The Reason for God: Belief in an Age of Skepticism
by Tim Keller (Riverhead, 2009)

Surprised by Scripture: Engaging Contemporary Issues
by N. T. Wright (HarperOne, 2014)
> **Author's Note:** This book will help you think through so much! From logical and scientific thinking around origin to the resurrection of Jesus to whether or not Jesus will actually return—and everything in between.

WEBSITES

www.testoffaith.com | Test of Faith
great videos and resources regarding science and faith

www.reasons.org | Reasons to Believe
resources from the intersection of faith and scientific thought

www.biologos.com | Biologos, Inc.
answers to questions about faith and science

http://goo.gl/Af8AqY | Peter Kreeft's "20 Arguments for God"
interesting (sometimes complicated) thoughts from a professor of philosophy

acknowledgments
Last Things

I want to thank these artists for their inspiration. Every word written flowed from their music. I listened and sang and typed furiously with them playing loudly in the background, so this was the soundtrack of the book:

Angels & Airwaves | *The Dream Walker*
Foo Fighters | *Sonic Highways*
for King and Country | *Run Wild. Live Free. Love Strong.*
311 | *Greatest Hits*
U2 | *Songs of Innocence*
Future of Forestry | *The Complete Travel Series*
(plus everything they've ever made)
Crowder | *Neon Steeple*

I also want to thank some of the most amazing people that I have ever met. First, Hanna, thank you for this incredible journey. It was super cool to go back and see the twists and turns of our conversations on—of all places—Facebook.

Also, a big shout out goes to these amazing people who contributed to the book:

Evan Jonokuchi
Heather Gordon
Troone Marchak
Jonny Mills
Zoe Morris
Krista Tilly
Casey Glickstein

Honestly, the best part of this book is what you said; it's what you wrote. I have loved our years together, and I pray there are many, many more. I just love you guys so much! Thank you for your openness, your hearts, your wisdom, and your willingness to stay in this adventure with Jesus!

Lastly, I want to thank my two favorite people in the world: Dancin and Kelsey—we are the Three Amigos!

To Dancin—thank you for being my daughter. I know that seems silly to say, but it is one of the greatest parts of my life! I love being your daddy and I watch you with such joy. It makes me want to do cartwheels.

And to Kelsey, my beautiful and lovely wife—I saw you twenty-four years ago and you took my breath away then. You still take my breath away. Thank you for being my best friend and life partner. I love this adventure called life that we are on, and I couldn't imagine a better teammate to have with me! Watching you grow and become the amazing person that you are has been such a privilege. Can't wait for Friday!

Made in the USA
Las Vegas, NV
05 May 2021

22505571R00148